ASIAN PICKLES AT HOME

ASIAN
PICKLES
AT HOME

75 EASY RECIPES FOR QUICK, FERMENTED, AND CANNED PICKLES

PAT TANUMIHARDJA

ROCKRIDGE
PRESS

Interior and Cover Designer: Lindsey Dekker

Art Producer: Janice Ackerman

Editor: Cecily McAndrews

Cover Photography: © 2020 Hélène Dujardin. Food Styling by Anna Hampton.

Interior Photography: p. x: © Antonis Achilleos/StockFood; p. 22: © Elisabeth von Pölnitz-Eisfeld/StockFood; p. 52: © Manuela Rüther/StockFood; p. 84: © Jan Wischnewski/StockFood; p. 120: © Alean Hrbková/StockFood.

Interior Illustration: © Microvector/Creative Market: pp. 5, 7, 25, 55, 85, 121.

Author Photo: © 2020 Sarah Culver.

ISBN: Print 978-1-64739-074-7 | eBook 978-1-64739-075-4

R0

For my mother, Julia.
Thank you for passing on excellent
culinary genes and for instilling in me
a love of cooking and eating good food.

CONTENTS

Introduction viii

CHAPTER 1: **Getting Started** 1

CHAPTER 2: **Fast and Fresh Pickles** 23

CHAPTER 3: **Chutneys, Sauces, and Seasonings** 53

CHAPTER 4: **Kimchi and Other Fermented Vegetables** 83

CHAPTER 5: **Pickling Outside the Box** 119

All About Altitude 149

Measurement Conversions 152

Resources 153

References 154

Recipes by Country 155

Index 157

INTRODUCTION

Growing up in Singapore with Indonesian Chinese parents, I was exposed to a whole gamut of pickles and fermented foods. Many of the pickles I grew up eating were akin to quick refrigerator pickles, vegetables like cucumbers, carrots, and perhaps some fiery bird chiles brined in a sweet-tart vinegar solution. These sweet-tart pickles added both crunch and heat to fried rice or noodles.

My mum also made the quintessential acar kuning, shredded vegetables tossed with a vinegary spice paste that is popular in Indonesia, Singapore, and Malaysia. She tossed pickled mustard cabbage into soup with sour plums and braised finely chopped pickled cabbage with pork belly. And, of course, no meal was complete without sambal. This assortment of chile pastes and dipping sauces is a flavor bomb, adding spice and savor to any dish.

Fermented foods like tempeh—fermented tofu—and taucheo—a fermented bean paste similar to miso—showed up regularly in our diet. In fact, one of my dad's favorite sweets was tape (pronounced ta-pay), which is fermented cassava.

Despite eating fermented foods all my life, I only learned about fermented vegetables like kimchi and sauerkraut when I moved to the United States to go to college. I had never considered fermenting on my own until someone gave me a kimchi recipe to include when I was writing *The Asian Grandmothers Cookbook*. Once I discovered how simple making kimchi was, I couldn't stop.

The bottom line is, if you're intimidated by Asian pickles, don't be. There will be a learning curve, but trust me, you really won't regret it. When you have preserved food on standby, you can easily assemble a healthy, delicious meal. Think of the various sweet, spicy, and sour *banchan* dishes at Korean restaurants that act as palate cleansers and complement the main dish. Toss pickles into stir-fries and soups, use them to top noodles and congee, stuff them into sandwiches—the possibilities are endless!

Though certainly not an exhaustive treatment, this book will cover in-depth the Asian countries and regions with long histories of preservation: Japan, Korea, China, India, and Southeast Asia. You'll discover that the techniques used (not to mention the flavors created) range from the universal vinegar-pickling and lactofermentation methods to more country-specific methods, like rice bran pickling and miso curing.

Canning isn't a popular tradition in Asia. Thus, Asian pickles typically rely on refrigeration or oil for preservation. That said, I still suggest several recipes that are suited for water-bath canning. So, if your refrigerator shelf is packed or you'd like to gift your creations, canning is an option for some of these recipes.

This book is not meant to be a definitive guide, because such a book would have to be hundreds of pages long. Instead, I offer a wide array of recipes, presenting you with an overview of the techniques and flavors you can create. Many of the recipes are traditional, while some are my more personalized modern takes which you can find in the Pickling Outside the Box chapter. Once you're comfortable with the basics, you can mix and match methods and ingredients to create a wide array of options to suit your taste buds.

Regardless of your pickling experience, I hope you'll find a recipe—or many—in this book that you'll love.

CHAPTER 1

Getting Started

Even if you've never pickled before, this book will show you how easy it is to get started. Pickling is simply a method of food preservation that involves marinating vegetables in a brine, made with either vinegar or salt. The marinating time depends on the method and can range from mere minutes to days or months. For pickling newbies, starting with quick pickles is probably the best route. You'll find lots of recipes to choose from in chapter 2.

Generally, pickling involves the following basic steps:

1. Wash your equipment with hot soapy water.
2. Prepare your vegetables.
3. Prepare your brine and spices.
4. Pack into jars and cover.
5. Wait!

WHAT IS A PICKLE?

Pickle is a noun and a verb. You can "pickle" just about any food to make it a "pickle," from a sauce to vegetables to eggs and fish. They're united under the "pickle" umbrella by what preserves them: salt (which is sometimes mixed with water to form a brine), acid (such as vinegar or citrus), and occasionally oil.

Fermenting is simply one type of pickling. The salty brine and healthy bacteria (lactobacilli) produce lactic acid during fermentation. This process can take anywhere from a few days to months. During fermentation, the chemical process expands and deepens existing flavors and adds new ones, all while providing the added benefits of probiotics.

Quick pickles (also called fresh or refrigerator pickles) can be eaten immediately after a quick bath in salt, sugar, and/or vinegar. Sometimes they need an extra few hours or a day or two to ripen. At this point, I'll take the opportunity to explore the different pickling techniques used in this book and briefly explain what distinguishes them and what unites them.

VINEGAR

Quick pickles like Pickled Daikon and Carrots (page 26) and Sweet-and-Sour Chinese Mustard Cabbage Pickle (page 30) are examples of vinegar pickles. The acetic acid in vinegar preserves food by increasing the acidity in the vegetables. This increase in acidity kills off any existing microorganisms, slows down decay, and helps prevent short-term spoilage.

Some vinegar-pickled foods can be eaten right away, but others will taste better after a longer bath to allow the flavors to develop. Either way, it still takes less time than fermentation.

Quick pickles last for 1 to 2 months in the refrigerator, if you can make them last that long. In general, vinegar-brined pickles are the best for canning. (I've added "Yes you can!" tips to recipes that are proven safe for canning.) Fermented foods, on the other hand, should not be canned, because the high heat used in canning kills the healthy bacteria produced during fermentation.

SALT

Not all salted pickles are fermented, but many of them are. Classic Cabbage Kimchi (page 86), Miso-Cured Daikon (page 29), and Salt-Pickled Vegetables (page 48) are examples of pickles that are preserved primarily with salt, though vinegar (or another acid) might also be an ingredient. Keep in mind that salty ingredients, like soy sauce or miso, can also preserve foods.

Salt draws water out of the vegetables being pickled and forms a brine that makes it harder for harmful bacteria to grow. Salt also acts as a preservative during this process by encouraging the growth of *Lactobacillus plantarum*. These probiotic "good" bacteria convert sugars into lactic acid, which preserves the produce and adds tanginess.

Temperature is also an important factor in the growth of good bacteria and proper fermentation. Optimum fermenting temperatures range between 65°F and 75°F. This range is slow enough for the complex flavors to develop while retaining the pickles' texture and allows you to enjoy the ferments within 2 to 6 weeks. Lactofermentation speeds up at warmer temperatures.

Fermented food does not need to be refrigerated. But the vegetables will continue to ferment and increase in sourness, so you might want to refrigerate them or store them in a cool location like the basement or the garage (in cooler climates) to significantly slow down the rate of fermentation. Fermented foods can be stored in the refrigerator for up to 3 months or even longer without losing their quality and good taste.

OIL

Indian pickles are often preserved using oil. Fiery Lime Pickle (page 70) and Green Mango Pickle (page 66) are two examples. Oil provides an airtight seal that can delay oxidation, prevent spoilage, and keep mold from growing. Mustard oil is the oil of choice in India for its spicy, wasabi-like flavor. I delve more deeply into this in Pickle Passport: India on page 54, but the sale of mustard oil for edible purposes is prohibited in the United States because it contains crucic acid, which is linked to cardiac damage in lab tests. I call for other oils in my recipes. Oil-preserved pickles last for 6 months at room temperature or up to 1 year in the refrigerator.

PLAYING NICE WITH SUGAR AND SPICE

Sugar and spices can have antimicrobial effects and thus help preserve food, too. Think of how sugar is used to preserve fruit and jams. Sugar gets a bad rap, but many of these recipes include just a little to mellow what would otherwise be a too-tart pickle, like Pickled Sunchokes (page 138).

In fact, many spices, such as clove, mustard seed, cinnamon, and cumin, have significant antibacterial and antifungal properties that help prevent food spoilage. In addition, pickles like Turmeric-Spiced Pickles (page 34) and Fiery Lime Pickle (page 70) get their distinctive flavor from these spices.

A QUICK HISTORY

Although its history is fuzzy, pickling is likely to have originated in the Indus Valley civilization in northwest India around 2400 BCE. The earliest mention of kimchi appears in Chinese poetry texts 3,000 years ago.

Pickling started off as a way to preserve nonseasonal food through the winter and for long journeys. Drying, the first method of preservation, worked well for meat and fish, but salting and fermenting vegetables became ideal for taste, texture, and nutrition.

Local ingredients and climate influenced the types of pickles that became popular, from chutneys in India to miso-pickled eggs in Japan. Take mangos, for instance. They are considered the national fruit of India and are beloved by many. It's not surprising that mangos were combined with a plethora of indigenous spices to make preserved foods like mango chutney and mango pickles. In Japan, miso and soy sauce are integral parts of the country's cuisine. Hence, they are also popular pickling agents. Pungency is valued in Korean cuisine, which is why you can find strong flavors in tangy kimchi and other fermented foods like soybean paste and chile paste. Thus, pickling is a delicious reflection of the culture and history of a given country.

INTRODUCING THE PICKLE PASSPORT

Throughout the book, you'll find a feature called the Pickle Passport. In these sections, you'll find a more detailed portrait of the pickling traditions in five different Asian countries and regions where pickling is a major component of the culinary history. You'll also find some must-try pickles, a rundown of the pickling techniques employed there, and extra information about how and when pickles are consumed. Consider it the Tour de Pickle! If you're interested in a specific country or region, here are the ones we discuss and the pages where you'll find them:

Japan, page 6

Southeast Asia, page 24

India, page 54

Korea, page 84

China, page 120

PICKLE PASSPORT: JAPAN

*Must-try pickles: Rice Bran Pickles (page 96), Pickled Ginger (page 42),
Salt-Pickled Vegetables (page 48), Miso-Cured Daikon (page 29)*

Of all the Asian countries, Japan has the most expansive range of pickling mediums and methods. They vary from a simple salting or vinegar brining to more complicated processes involving cultured molds and fermentation.

In Japan, the term *tsukemono* refers to all preserved or fermented foods. In the days before refrigeration, pickling was used as a method to preserve food, and some traditionally prepared pickles can be kept almost indefinitely. While the origins of tsukemono are unclear, it is not surprising that preserving food in salt or saltwater is a longstanding practice. Japan is an archipelago surrounded by the ocean, after all. More specifically, the *Engi-shiki*, or *Procedures of the Engi Era,* a compilation of administrative rules created in the 10th century, listed different varieties of tsukemono and the best ways to make them. Pickling methods were developed at that time to store food to prevent famine in times of poor harvest, to preserve extra food during abundant harvests, and to improve the flavor of food.

Tsukemono are usually made from popular local produce like daikon radishes, cucumbers, eggplant, carrots, cabbage, ginger, and plums (ume). Sometimes seaweed and seafood are added to pickle mixtures for flavor and variety. Tsukemono are an essential part of the Japanese meal, served alongside rice and miso soup because they add color, texture, and taste as a relish, condiment, or palate cleanser. In addition, they provide probiotics, vitamins,

and minerals. They are also often eaten at the end of a meal to aid digestion.

The simplest pickling method is to salt vegetables before massaging them and draining any liquids. These pickles can be eaten immediately. On the other end of the spectrum is the traditional Japanese technique of fermenting vegetables in a pickling bed that can take weeks to prepare. Pickling beds can be used for pickling all manner of vegetables, from cucumbers to eggplant, and they produce pickles ranging from mild to pungent, depending on how long the vegetables spend "in bed."

The first step is to make a fermented bed that forms the medium for the pickling bed, which is usually made from roasted rice bran or rice koji, cooked rice that's been inoculated with the mold *Aspergillus oryzae* (see page 104). Roasted rice bran is the most common, and it is usually combined with spices and aromatics like garlic, ginger, and chile peppers, as well as dried shiitakes or sardines to add umami. Vegetable scraps are also added to promote fermentation. After about two weeks, the pickling bed is ready.

After all that work, it's good that you can reuse a bed indefinitely, provided you maintain it—for more on this, check out the Rice Bran Pickles on page 96.

PICKLES AND YOUR HEALTH

Pickles have long been revered for their health benefits. They are fat-free and low in calories, contain beneficial bacteria that can promote gut health, contain a variety of other vitamins, and have health benefits that range from lowering your risk of heart disease to improving digestion.

PICKLING AND NUTRIENTS

According to a UC Davis study, both fermented and quick pickles still possess many of the vitamins and antioxidants present in raw vegetables. Vinegar used in the pickling process can also lower insulin levels and improve digestion. Just pay attention to the salt content of pickles (see "But What About Salt and Sugar?" on page 9).

PROBIOTICS

Fermented pickles contained probiotics long before they were cool. Essentially, probiotics are live bacteria that support the beneficial microorganisms in your gut. They help improve your digestive health and support your immune system.

When vegetables are preserved with salt, such as in Miso-Ginger Sauerkraut (page 114) and Sichuan Pickles (page 110), they undergo a process called lacto-fermentation. During this process, bad bacteria are killed off by the saltiness of the brine and the good, lactic-acid-producing bacteria (primarily *Lactobacillus* genus) thrive. These good bacteria are the probiotics in the final ferment that contribute to good health.

Other probiotic-rich foods include kefir, kombucha, and miso.

MORE VEGETABLES ON YOUR PLATE

Pickles are so tasty you'll want to eat more of them, which means more fruits and vegetables in your diet. Pickles are delicious straight from the jar and can make healthy staples, like whole grains and produce, more appealing. The zesty sweet-sourness and awesome crunch you get from pickling make foods that you may not have loved before into lovable favorites, and the flavor and zing make old favorites come to life even more. Pickled mustard cabbage on red curry noodles? Pickled cucumbers with fried rice? Lime pickle with rice and meat? Yes, yes, and yes!

Salt is essential to food preservation and makes up about 5 to 10 percent of most pickling recipes. When fermenting, stick to the amount called for. If you use too little, your ferment might come out mushy or moldy. If you're concerned about your salt intake, eat fermented pickles in moderation.

The good news is that in most quick pickle recipes that are eaten immediately or items that will eventually be refrigerated, you can alter the amount of salt and sugar to taste. Additionally, you can reduce the amount of salt in any recipe that is not salt brined or lactofermented, including vinegar-brined pickles that you intend to can. Likewise, many of the recipes use sugar as a way to balance flavor. Feel free to adjust amounts to your liking. There are exceptions, though, such as Thai Sweet Chile Sauce (page 62), where that amount of sugar is needed to thicken and preserve it.

In any event, I have tried to include the minimum amounts of salt and sugar needed to make the recipes work just right. I also indicate where they can be eliminated or reduced according to your personal taste.

USING THE RIGHT INGREDIENTS

Using the right ingredients when pickling can make the difference between a crisp, tasty pickle and a soft, bland one. To ensure a successful pickle, choose your ingredients very carefully, from using the right type of salt (essential!) to buying the freshest produce you can get your hands on.

The water you use can also make a difference. The minerals and chlorine in hard water can interfere with pickling, so soft water is ideal. Whether you have hard or soft water depends on where you live. Higher mineral content, mainly calcium and magnesium, makes water hard. Soft water tends to have higher concentrations of sodium. You can make water softer by installing a water-softening system that reduces the water's mineral concentration. Some die-hard picklers use distilled water, but if you're comfortable drinking the water, it's probably fine to use for pickling.

SALT

As I mentioned, salt is critical for fermenting and for flavor. The balance of salt to vegetable during fermentation is very important. Too little salt, and the good bacteria won't develop. Too much salt, and the food may ferment too quickly, creating a mushy ferment and/or allowing mold to grow.

Basic guidelines (by weight) are 2 to 5 percent salt to vegetables/fruits. The lower end (2 percent) is suited to softer produce like leafy greens, and the higher end (5 percent) to harder produce like cucumbers.

The following are the best salts to use for pickling.

Sea Salt

I usually buy natural sea salt from Asian markets, where it is sometimes labeled kimchi salt. Look for crystals similar in size to kosher salt. This is the salt I use for all of the recipes in this book.

Canning and Pickling Salt

Canning or pickling salt is pure granulated salt. Unlike table salt, it doesn't contain iodine and anti-caking agents, which can create off flavors and cause the pickling liquid to turn cloudy. Canning salt is finer than coarse sea salt or kosher salt and dissolves much faster. That's why it is often the salt of choice (though not compulsory) for canning enthusiasts.

Kosher Salt

Kosher salt has large crystals, which do not dissolve as quickly as pickling salt. The top two brands, Morton and Diamond Crystal, have different crystal sizes. Diamond Crystal's grains are coarser and result in more space between the salt crystals, so it is less salty per tablespoon than Morton's finer crystals. Diamond Crystal kosher salt is a good substitute for sea salt in the recipes in this cookbook.

VINEGAR

Vinegar is an essential ingredient for quick pickling, because the acetic acid it contains preserves the pickles. *If you're canning your pickles, it is essential to use a vinegar that has at least 5 percent acidity.* This ensures that low-acid vegetables like cucumbers are properly acidified and are safe for canning; check the label to be sure. For quick pickles, the basic brine is equal parts vinegar and water. You can adjust the ratio to use more vinegar (i.e., ⅔ vinegar: ⅓ water) but not less. Add sugar if the flavor is too harsh.

Rice Vinegar

Rice vinegar is made from fermented rice. It has a mild, slightly sweet flavor and is a staple ingredient in Asian cooking. This is my vinegar of choice, and my favorite brand is Marukan. Rice vinegar is diluted to an acidity of between 4 and 4.3 percent, meaning it is not suitable for canning. Substitute apple cider vinegar or white wine vinegar if you plan on canning your pickles.

Distilled White Vinegar

While close in color to rice vinegar, white vinegar is sharp and harsh in comparison. I think it's the most aggressive of the vinegars, but it's inexpensive for pickling in bulk. Use more sugar to counter the sharper flavor.

Apple Cider Vinegar

Apple cider vinegar has a mild flavor that I think is the best substitute for rice vinegar. Keep in mind, however, that it causes produce to darken.

PRODUCE

When making pickles, it's important to use the best produce you can find. Buy vegetables in season and locally where possible because they're fresher and less costly. This means that farmers' markets are an ideal place to buy produce for pickling.

In this book, I try to use produce that's easy to find, but there are a few items that are most likely available only at Asian markets. If you're shopping for more unusual vegetables, it's best to go to an Asian market where there's a higher turnover. Of course, this isn't possible for everyone, so just buy the best you can find, avoiding anything with bruises or mold.

Chiles

I use fresh long red chiles in my recipe for Thai Sweet Chile Sauce (page 62); I also use small bird or Thai chiles. You can use Korean chiles, Anaheim chiles, or Fresnos (red jalapeños). For green chiles, use chiles labeled Korean green chiles at the Asian market or jalapeños and serranos.

Citrus

Feel free to use supermarket lemons and limes for the recipes in this book. You may also choose Key limes, which are similar to the small limes in Asia.

Cucumbers

My choice are Persian cucumbers. Short and narrow, they are dense and thin skinned with almost no watery seeds. Short and squat kirby cucumbers are another pickling favorite. English cucumbers don't hold up as well but work for quick pickles.

Eggplant

Long, slender Japanese and Chinese varieties of eggplant are ideal for the recipes in this book. If you can find them, use golf-ball-size green and white Thai baby eggplants for Sweet and Spicy Pickled Baby Eggplant (page 36), or fairy tale or baby Italian eggplants.

Mangos

Indian pickles use green mangos bred specially for pickling, but unripe Kent or Tommy Atkins mangos that are very firm and uniformly green skinned will work.

Papaya

Green, unripe papayas are used for making Shredded Vegetable Pickles (page 50). They are usually available at Asian markets and specifically labeled as green papaya. Substitute the firmest papayas you can find, green apples, or kohlrabi.

SPICES

Most of the spices I use in this book are available at your local supermarket or at least at a specialty market like Whole Foods. Here are a few of the less common ones, which you might need to seek out at an Asian market.

Gochujaru

Gochujaru is made of ground Korean chile peppers, and it gives kimchi its heat and color while keeping it from souring too quickly. It has a heat level between cayenne and paprika, with the smokiness of chipotle. It's available at Asian markets finely and coarsely ground. Finely ground is best for making Korean Red Pepper Paste (page 80), and coarsely ground is used for making kimchi.

Curry Leaves

Curry leaves come from the curry tree and have nothing to do with curry powder. They have a unique musky fragrance and are used whole to flavor chutneys and sambals. As many as 20 small bright green leaves may be attached to a slender stem. Find them at Indian or Asian markets, either fresh or frozen.

Asafoetida

This pungent, resinous gum is commonly sold as a coarsely ground powder. It is used mainly in Indian cooking, in chutney and pickle recipes.

Fenugreek Seeds

Fenugreek leaves and seeds are popular in Indian cooking. You'll use these seeds, which offer a nutty, maple syrup taste, in the pickle and chutney recipes in chapter 3.

Several recipes in this book use specialized ingredients like fish sauce and miso. These ingredients add umami, which is often called the sixth taste. If you can't find them, don't worry—your pickle will still be tasty.

Fish Sauce

Fish sauce is made by salting and fermenting fish (often anchovies) and then pressing them to release an amber liquid. It lends a salty, umami-rich flavor to recipes like Roasted Chile Jam (page 56) and Lemongrass Chile Sauce (page 78). I use Red Boat brand, but Three Crabs and Squid brands are also reliable.

Miso

Miso is a fermented condiment typically made from soybeans, rice, and barley. The most common varieties are white, yellow, and red, and they vary according to the ratio of ingredients, how long they're fermented, and the salt and koji (a type of beneficial mold) content. (For more on koji, see Salted Rice Koji Pickles, page 104.) In general, though, white miso is the mildest and red is the strongest. What you pick depends on your preference. I use a mild white miso in most of my recipes because it's the most versatile.

Kombu

This seaweed is sold in dried sheets and is often labeled dried kelp or dashi kombu. It smells and tastes of the sea and is a main ingredient in dashi, the Japanese fish and seaweed stock that is used in everything from miso soup to braises like sukiyaki. Emerald Cove is a commonly available brand sold at supermarkets.

Soy Sauce

For pickling purposes, I use Japanese shoyu, which is thicker and sweeter than Chinese soy sauce. I like San-J or Kikkoman brands. Use tamari for a gluten-free option.

Rice Flour

Many kimchi recipes use a paste made from rice flour and water. The rice paste adds body and encourages the growth of the right bacteria. I generally use sweet rice flour in my recipes, but you can use any type of rice flour.

OUTFIT YOUR KITCHEN

You don't need fancy equipment to start pickling and fermenting. In fact, you probably already have most of the essential tools.

KITCHEN SCALE

Correct proportions are very important for a safe fermentation process, so please use a kitchen scale to accurately weigh ingredients when called for. This is especially important when the amount of salt in a brine is a percentage of the weight of vegetables you're pickling (such as in Miso-Ginger Sauerkraut, page 114).

NONREACTIVE POTS, PANS, AND UTENSILS

Use stainless steel or enameled pans and avoid cast iron. These metals will not react with acid or salt and will not affect the quality and safety of your pickles.

WEIGHTS

Weights keeps fermenting foods submerged in brine. You can buy special fermenting weights, but small glass jars and glass or porcelain dinner/pie plates work just as well. Another option is to fill a food-grade plastic bag with brine (to prevent dilution just in case the bag breaks—use 1 tablespoon salt per cup of water). Vegetable scraps, especially the root bottoms of cabbages, work great, too.

JARS AND CROCKS

No matter what type of pickles you make, select food-safe containers, preferably glass or ceramic. Do not use plastic, which might leach chemicals or stain. Generally, you will need a 1-gallon container for every 5 pounds of fresh vegetables.

LIDS

Lids should fit your jars and not be rusty or bent. If you're canning, do not reuse lids. It is okay to reuse rings.

LARGE BOWLS

Select glass or ceramic bowls for salting and mixing kimchi. Don't use plastic, because it might stain.

WATER-BATH CANNING EQUIPMENT

This is only necessary if you're planning on canning your pickles. See page 16 for a full rundown.

SPICE GRINDER OR MORTAR AND PESTLE

Spices add wonderful flavor to pickles. It's useful to have a spice grinder or mortar and pestle at home. You can buy ground spices, but I prefer to buy whole spices and toast them just before grinding them down to a powder myself. Whole spices retain their fragrance and flavor longer.

CANNING ASIAN PICKLES

Canning stops fermentation and the growth of bacteria that cause spoilage. While canning is not a traditional practice in Asian food culture, there are several recipes in this cookbook that can be canned. High-acid, nonfermented foods like pickles soaked in vinegar, chutneys, and sauces are suitable for water-bath canning and should be canned as soon as they're ready. Unfortunately, the high heat required in canning destroys the probiotics and other good bacteria developed during fermentation, so don't can your ferments. Throughout this book, I have indicated many of the recipes that can be canned with "Yes you can!" tips. Here is a full list of recipes that are able to be canned:

- Pickled Daikon and Carrots, page 26
- Mum's Mixed Pickle, page 37
- Thai Sweet Chile Sauce, page 62
- Mango Chutney, page 63
- Plum Sauce (or Duck Sauce), page 73
- Banana Ketchup, page 74
- Asian Pear and Fennel Pickles, page 124
- Pickled Sunchokes, page 138
- Chinese Five-Spice Pickled Grapes, page 144

HOW TO CAN

If it's your first time canning, don't be nervous! Here's a step-by-step guide. Before you start, it's important to check the altitude charts in the appendix (page 149), because you might have to adjust the canning time if you live at high elevation.

Read Your Recipe

Before you begin, make sure you have all the correct ingredients weighed out to ensure the right proportions. If any of your ratios are off, your produce won't be properly pickled. Additionally, lay out all the tools you might need. Here's a list:

- Glass mason jars (the easiest to find are Ball or Kerr)
- Oven mitts
- Jar lifter with rubber grips
- Jar lids (sealing metal discs) and bands (the threaded metal rings that hold down the lids)
- Common kitchen items like a wooden spoon, spatula, ladle, and kitchen towel
- Large, deep stock pot with a tight-fitting lid (when all the jars are inside, you must have room for 1 inch of boiling water over the lids)
- Canning rack (or any rack that will fit in your canner/pot)

Make the Food

While there's room for experimentation (especially with flavorings), it's best to follow the recipe exactly until you get the hang of it. Don't boil pickles with vinegar for too long, as that might let too much of the vinegar boil off and throw off the pH balance of the pickles.

Prep the Jars and Lids

If you're processing food for less than 10 minutes, you'll need to sterilize your jars. Otherwise, your jars should just be clean. The easiest way to sterilize your jars and lids is by using the sterilizing cycle in your dishwasher. This will also keep them warm and prevent breakage due to an abrupt change in temperature when you place the jars in your canning pot. If you don't have a dishwasher, boil water-filled jars on a rack in a large stockpot for 10 minutes. Boil the lids separately.

Fill Your Jars

Fill your jars so they have the right headspace (½ inch for most items), then remove bubbles by sliding a rubber spatula between the jar and the food to release trapped air. Clean the rims and jars of residue. Adjust the lid on each jar, apply the band, and twist just until you encounter resistance; don't overtighten the jars.

Place the filled jar in the canner. Repeat until all jars are used or the canner is full. Make sure the water covers the jars by at least 1 inch. Place the lid on the canner and bring the water to a full rolling boil.

Process the Jars

When the water boils, set a timer for the recommended time. Adjust the heat until the water maintains a rolling boil for the entire processing time. When the time is up, remove the lid and allow to cool for 5 minutes before removing the jars from the canner. Set the jars on a rack or towel for 12 to 24 hours.

Check the Seal

Press each lid in the center. They should not flex up and down. Remove the bands and try to lift the lids off. If the lids can't come off, they have a good seal.

FERMENTING ASIAN PICKLES

Fermentation or lactofermentation occurs when naturally occurring good bacteria called probiotics transform sugars in fruits and vegetables into lactic acid to create delicious, tangy ferments.

Initially, salt inhibits the growth of bad bacteria and prevents spoilage. Within a few days, the probiotics take over to keep the ferment safe from toxins and food spoilers. The probiotics also break down larger compounds into smaller molecules, amplifying existing flavors, adding depth of flavor, and creating new flavors.

In general, three methods are used: dry-salted (sauerkraut method), brined, and kimchi-style (which incorporates both). In Asian cultures, brined and kimchi-style are the most common.

This book has an entire chapter on fermented pickles, but you will also find them in other chapters, including chapters 3 and 5.

HOW TO FERMENT

Fermenting isn't hard, plus you don't need any fancy equipment. All that's required are a fermenting vessel, fresh produce, and salt. You must follow certain steps to do it correctly, though. But don't worry, it will all be worth it in the end. You will be rewarded with a tasty and healthy product you can be proud of!

Clean Your Crock or Jar

Simply wash your vessel with soap and hot water. Sterilizing is unnecessary, because bad bacteria can't survive in the acidic and anaerobic environment created during fermentation.

Prepare the Recipe

Follow a tested recipe and prepare all the required ingredients and equipment before starting.

Cut your ingredients into even sizes so that they ferment at an equal rate. The smaller the pieces, the more exposed surface area and the faster the ferment. Grating works well for hard or crunchy vegetables like carrots. Firm vegetables such as daikon radish can be sliced very thinly, while softer vegetables such as eggplant or greens should be cut into larger pieces to preserve their shape during fermentation.

Always use the right amount of salt called for, paying attention to whether finer pickling or coarser kosher salt is used. The balance of salt to vegetables during fermenting is very important. Too little salt and the good bacteria won't develop. Too much salt and the food may ferment too quickly, creating a mushy ferment and/or allowing mold to grow.

Weight the Ferment

The key to a successful ferment is to maintain an oxygen-free environment. It is very important to weigh down your ferment to keep it submerged beneath the brine. Sealing your vessel is also key. If the ferment is exposed to air, it will allow mold to grow. I've discussed the different types of weights you can use on page 14.

Wait for It ...

A ferment can take anywhere from 1 day to 6 weeks to be ready. It all depends on the ambient temperature (65°F to 75°F is ideal) and the time of year. The cooler it is, the longer it will take to ferment. If the ambient temperature is higher than 75°F, it will ferment too quickly and may lack flavor and/or turn moldy.

Burping/Releasing Gas

For the first few days, the bad bacteria from your ferment will produce a lot of carbon dioxide. Loosen or open the lid of your vessel at least once a day to release the built-up pressure. This is called "burping." If you can, store your ferment in a dark, undisturbed place such as a kitchen cabinet or pantry.

Decant Your Ferment

Once the vegetable is fermented to your liking, move it to cold storage. You can divide it up into smaller containers if you'd like. Always use a clean utensil to scoop out your ferment to avoid introducing new bacteria. In general, a ferment will keep in the refrigerator for a few months, but it will continue to ferment and get sour. After 2 or 3 months, it may be too sour to eat straight out of the jar.

THE SECRET INGREDIENT: TIME

Curing or fermenting takes time because time is crucial for allowing flavors to develop and probiotics to proliferate. Quick pickles can be eaten immediately, while other vinegar pickles may take a couple of hours to a day or two to be tasty. Fermented foods can take anywhere from 2 weeks (Fiery Lime Pickle, page 70) to 2 months (Korean Red Pepper Paste, page 80) to be ready.

Most pickles should be cured or fermented at room temperature before being refrigerated, but this timing is arbitrary. The only way to really know when a ferment is ready is to taste it. When it tastes pleasant to the person who will be eating it, it's time to make the move to cold storage.

WHAT'S THAT SMELL?

Fermenting inevitably releases strong odors, especially when you're working with pungent flavors.

Other than experience, there's no foolproof way to tell whether something is good-smelly or . . . well, bad-smelly. The best way to tell whether a fermented food has gone bad is to look for visual clues and to taste it. If you see colored mold (see page 20) or the food tastes off to you, then you should throw it out. You can rest assured that intentionally fermented foods, though smelly, are not actually spoiled. They are salted to prevent them from spoiling, flavored to make them tasty, and kept in an anaerobic environment (no oxygen means no rotting).

To mitigate the smell, store fermenting foods in the garage, the basement, or the back of an empty kitchen cabinet. Asian markets have special containers with tight seals for this purpose. You can also pull plastic wrap tightly over the mouth of your jar before putting the lid on. If all else fails, dig a hole in your backyard and bury your ferment underground like they do in Korea!

HOW TO KNOW IF SOMETHING IS WRONG

Pickling and fermenting can be a tricky process. The following chart highlights typical problems, causes, and solutions to help you solve any issues that arise.

PROBLEM	CAUSE	CAN I STILL EAT THE PICKLE?	WHAT TO DO
White film develops	Harmless kahm yeast	Yes	Lift the film off and discard. When ready to refrigerate, transfer the ferment to a new jar with as little headspace as possible.
Mold appears on vegetables or brine surface	The ferment isn't fully submerged and is exposed to oxygen. The wrong salt ratio was used. The vegetables and/or tools weren't clean.	In general, toss	However, if only a few spots of white mold appear, it's okay to simply lift off the mold and eat the food. If more than a few spots, toss. Any other color mold besides white, toss. Minimize mold by using a weight and a fermentation seal.
Sauce or brine gets fizzy	Carbon dioxide gas is a natural byproduct of fermentation.	Yes	Burp your jar regularly. Use a jar with self-burping fermentation seals or a water lock.
Black stuff in the middle of ferment	Air pockets of oxygen/ not an airtight seal	Toss	Pack your food more tightly next time. Make sure your jar or crock is sealed properly.
Ferment is soft and mushy	There is not enough salt in the brine. Salt rids vegetables of moisture and keeps things crispy.	Yes, but it might not taste good.	Make sure you have the appropriate amount of salt in your brine.
Kimchi is slimy	Too much sugar or rice paste was used.	Yes, but it might not taste good.	Make sure you maintain the right balance of salt to sugar. Either use less or skip altogether. (Rice paste is not always necessary for kimchi making.)

PICKLED DAIKON AND CARROTS / DO CHUA, PAGE 26

CHAPTER 2

Fast and Fresh Pickles

Pickled Daikon and Carrots | Do Chua 26

Quick Cucumber and Carrot Pickles 27

Sweet Cucumber Pickles | Hua Gua 28

Miso-Cured Daikon | Misozuke 29

Sweet-and-Sour Chinese Mustard Cabbage Pickle 30

Pineapple and Cucumber Relish | Acar Nenas Dan Timun 31

Indonesian Fruit Salad | Asinan Buah 32

Soy-Pickled Mushrooms 33

Turmeric-Spiced Pickles | Acar Kuning 34

Sweet and Spicy Pickled Baby Eggplant 36

Mum's Mixed Pickle | Acar Campur 37

Spicy Smacked Cucumbers | Suan La Pai Huang Gua 38

Sliced Papaya Pickles 40

Sesame Zucchini Threads | Hobak Namul 41

Pickled Ginger | Gari 42

Pickled Bean Sprouts | Du'a Giá 44

Sesame Pickled Cabbage 45

Pickled Green Chiles 46

Spicy Pickled Lotus Root 47

Salt-Pickled Vegetables | Shiozuke 48

Shredded Vegetable Pickles | Achara 50

PICKLE PASSPORT: SOUTHEAST ASIA

*Must-try pickles: Pickled Daikon and Carrots (page 26),
Turmeric-Spiced Pickles (page 34), Shredded Vegetable Pickles (page 50),
Sweet and Spicy Pickled Baby Eggplant (page 36)*

As in many parts of the world, pickling in Southeast Asia (including Indonesia, Malaysia, the Philippines, Myanmar, Vietnam, Singapore, and Thailand) started as a way to prevent foods from spoiling quickly, especially in the intense heat and humidity of the tropics. People added spices like chiles and turmeric because they are abundant and they inhibit bacteria growth, which explains why Southeast Asian pickles are so flavorful. Today, the seasonings for local pickles run the gamut from garlic, ginger, and red chiles to lemongrass and lime leaves (makrut in Thai).

When it comes to the question of what gets pickled in Southeast Asia, the answer is everything. From vegetables and fruit to fish and meat, anything edible is pickled. Common vegetables like cucumbers, carrots, and daikon radishes are popular for pickling, as are tropical fruits like papayas, pineapple, and mangos.

In Southeast Asia, vinegar-brined pickles are universally popular. Vinegar-to-water-to-sugar and salt ratios vary from culture to culture, region to region. Migrants from India and China

also brought with them pickles that have been adapted to local ingredients and palates over the centuries. Acar or achar—popular in Indonesia, Malaysia, and Singapore—is a localized version of Indian achaar (try Turmeric-Spiced Pickles, the Indonesian version, on page 34 and Fiery Lime Pickle, the Indian version, on page 70). This pickle is made with a basic Indian-influenced spice paste and gussied up with indigenous ingredients like candlenuts, galangal, and/or palm sugar. Originally from China, Sweet-and-Sour Chinese Mustard Cabbage Pickle (page 30) shows up in Thai and Singaporean cuisine, both as a condiment and cooked into dishes. Other fermented foods include tape (pronounced "ta-pay"), fermented cassava that's eaten as a sweet snack in Indonesia, and fermented eggplant in Vietnam.

Pickles are eaten as a refreshing snack on a hot, sunny day. Additionally, they add texture and flavor to many Southeast Asian grilled meat and fish dishes, satays in particular. Pickles also accompany rice and noodle dishes to add heat and crunch.

PICKLED DAIKON AND CARROTS | DO CHUA

VIETNAM

Makes: 2 pints | **Prep and Cook time:** 30 minutes, plus 30 minutes salting time | **Curing time:** 1 hour

1 pound daikon radish, peeled and cut into matchsticks (1 large daikon)

1 pound carrots, peeled and cut into matchsticks (5 medium carrots)

2 teaspoons fine sea salt

1 cup water

1 cup rice vinegar

½ cup sugar

1 tablespoon coarse sea salt or kosher salt

2 small dried red chiles, like chiles de arbol (optional)

Traditionally stuffed into banh mi sandwiches or tossed over vermicelli noodle bowls, this pickled duo of daikon and carrot is very popular in Vietnamese cuisine. This recipe makes a sweeter pickle, but you can use less sugar if you like. Start with ¼ cup sugar and add more to taste, and feel free to adjust the ratio of daikon to carrot, too.

1. In a large bowl, toss the daikon and carrot with the fine sea salt and set aside until the vegetables are soft and pliable, about 30 minutes. This process draws out moisture and allows the pickling brine to penetrate the vegetables for better texture and flavor.

2. Meanwhile, in a medium saucepan over medium-high heat, combine the water, vinegar, sugar, and coarse sea salt. Bring to a boil, stirring until the sugar and salt dissolve completely. Set aside to cool.

3. Rinse the vegetables and drain. Pack them into 2 pint-size jars and add one dried chile per jar, if using. Divide the brine between the jars. Seal and refrigerate. Steep for at least 1 hour before eating. The pickles will keep in the refrigerator for 4 weeks.

YES YOU CAN! While it's not traditional, this pickle can be canned so it keeps for up to a year on the shelf. Double the quantity of vegetables and salt, and make the brine with 3 cups water, 3 cups *distilled* white vinegar (do not use rice vinegar, because its acidity level is not suitable for canning), and 1½ cups sugar. Following the canning instructions on page 15, place the salted vegetables in 6 pint-size jars that have been washed with hot, soapy water. Fill the jars with hot brine, leaving a ½-inch headspace. Remove any air bubbles, wipe the rims, and seal the jars. Process in a water-bath canner for 10 minutes. Wait 5 minutes before removing the jars, and check the seals after 12 to 24 hours.

QUICK CUCUMBER AND CARROT PICKLES

CHINA

Makes: 1 pint | **Prep time:** 10 minutes, plus salting time | **Curing time:** 15 minutes to 1 hour

2 large seedless cucumbers
(8 to 9 inches long)
1 medium carrot, peeled and
cut into thin rounds
1¼ teaspoons coarse sea salt
or kosher salt, divided
½ cup rice vinegar
½ cup water
¼ cup sugar
2 tablespoons maple syrup
2 (⅛-inch-thick) slices peeled
fresh ginger
1 garlic clove, smashed
Pinch dried chili flakes

My friend's mother taught me how to make this simple pickle. After moving to the United States, she started replacing ginger syrup with maple syrup and some fresh ginger slices. I like cutting the cucumbers into long flat ribbons. With such a large exposed surface area, the cucumber absorbs the brine readily and quickly—and it looks pretty.

1. Trim and halve each cucumber lengthwise. Place one half flat-side down on your cutting board and, using a vegetable peeler (a "Y"-peeler works great), slice the cucumber lengthwise into paper-thin strips. Repeat with the remaining cucumber.

2. Put the cucumber slices and carrots in a colander and toss with 1 teaspoon of salt. Let them sit in the sink while you prepare the brine.

3. In a small bowl, mix together the vinegar, water, sugar, maple syrup, ginger, garlic, chili flakes, and remaining ¼ teaspoon of salt. Microwave on medium-high for 30 seconds, until the mixture is warm. Stir until the sugar dissolves completely. Taste and adjust the seasonings if desired. Let the brine cool.

4. Rinse the vegetables and shake dry. In a large bowl, toss the vegetables and brine together. Let stand for at least 15 minutes in the refrigerator but preferably 1 hour.

TRY IT WITH: This cool, crisp, and mildly sweet pickle perks up fried rice or noodles.

SWEET CUCUMBER PICKLES | HUA GUA

TAIWAN

Makes: 1 pint | **Prep time:** 10 minutes, plus 1 hour salting time | **Curing time:** 24 hours

1 pound small seedless
 cucumbers, like Persian (6 to
 8 cucumbers)

1 tablespoon sugar,
 plus 2 teaspoons

1½ teaspoons coarse sea salt
 or kosher salt, divided

1 tablespoon Chinese
 black vinegar

1 tablespoon regular soy sauce

2 teaspoons dark soy sauce

3 garlic cloves, smashed
 and peeled

1 star anise pod

Soy-pickled cucumbers are very common across the Far East. This Taiwanese version uses Chinese black vinegar (see the ingredient tip that follows), regular (also called light) soy sauce, and dark soy sauce, which give this pickle its dark appearance and particular sweet-tart flavor. Dark soy sauce is less salty than regular soy sauce and has a touch of sweetness. If you can't find it, substitute 1½ teaspoons regular soy sauce plus ½ teaspoon molasses.

1. Halve each cucumber crosswise and then cut into 4 equal sections. In a medium bowl, toss the slices with 2 teaspoons of sugar and 1 teaspoon of salt. Refrigerate for 1 hour.

2. Meanwhile, in a small bowl, make the sauce by combining the remaining 1 tablespoon of sugar, the remaining ½ teaspoon of salt, and the black vinegar, regular soy sauce, dark soy sauce, garlic, and star anise. Stir until the sugar and salt dissolve completely. Taste and adjust the seasonings if desired.

3. After 1 hour in the refrigerator, the cucumbers should have released at least ¼ cup of liquid. Drain and discard the liquid and add the prepared sauce. Toss to mix. Cover and marinate in the refrigerator for 24 hours. These pickles will keep for 1 week in the refrigerator.

INGREDIENT TIP: Chinese black vinegar is a specialty vinegar made from glutinous rice and malt and is widely used in Chinese cuisine. It is also called Chinkiang vinegar, after the city that is famous for its production. Chinese black vinegar is somewhat mild with a hint of sweetness and has a complexity similar to balsamic vinegar. Use it in stir-fries and dipping sauces. You can substitute balsamic vinegar or white rice vinegar if you can't find it in your local markets.

MISO-CURED DAIKON | MISOZUKE

JAPAN

Makes: 1 pint | **Prep time:** 10 minutes, plus 1 hour salting time | **Curing time:** 2 to 3 hours

1 pound daikon radish,
  peeled and cut into
  1-by-2-inch pieces
2 tablespoons sugar
2 teaspoons salt
¼ cup white or red miso
2 teaspoons mirin

Just about any food can be cured with miso, from vegetables to fish. This curing method makes an umami-rich, mildly salty pickle that tastes great with rice and fish or on its own. Miso-cured daikon is very common, but you can try this curing method with other vegetables, like carrots, cucumbers, and eggplant. Remember that thin, soft vegetables (like eggplant and cucumber) cure faster than thick, tough vegetables (like radish and carrot). Thinner, smaller pieces pickle faster, too. Also keep in mind that red miso is saltier than white and requires a shorter curing time. Adjust according to which miso you prefer.

1. In a zip-top bag, toss the daikon with the sugar and salt. Remove as much air as possible and seal. Refrigerate for 1 hour, weighing the daikon down with something heavy like a glass container or milk jug. This keeps the daikon immersed in the dry brine and facilitates the release of moisture.

2. Drain the daikon and rinse. Drain any liquids from the bag. Add the miso and mirin to the bag and massage into the daikon. Refrigerate for 2 to 3 hours. Taste to see whether the pickle is pleasant to your taste. It should taste a little salty, sweet, and sour. Cure for longer if desired.

3. Rub off the miso paste from the daikon before serving. These pickles will keep for 1 week in the refrigerator.

   TRY IT WITH: You can reuse the miso marinade several times (it will remain flavorful for up to 1 month). Once it loses most of its flavor, you can still cook with it. Try it in a stir-fry or a soup.

SWEET-AND-SOUR CHINESE MUSTARD CABBAGE PICKLE

CHINA

Makes: 2 pints | **Prep and Cook time:** 10 minutes, plus sitting time | **Curing time:** 2 to 5 days

2 pounds Chinese mustard
    cabbage, cut into bite-size
    pieces (2 medium cabbages)
½ cup water
½ cup distilled white vinegar
½ cup sugar
1 tablespoon coarse sea salt or
    kosher salt
1 (½-inch) piece fresh ginger,
    peeled and cut into 4 slices

This pickle is a variation on the fermented salted cabbage that is popular in many Asian cuisines. Steeped in a sweet-and-sour vinegar brine, this mustard cabbage pickle is ready to eat in 2 days, rather than the weeks it takes for the fermented version.

1. Bring a large pot of water to a boil over medium-high heat. Add the cabbage, stirring until it darkens, 2 to 3 minutes. Drain and let cool.

2. In a small saucepan over medium-high heat, combine the water, vinegar, sugar, and salt. Bring to a boil, stirring until the salt and sugar dissolve completely. Remove from the heat and let cool.

3. Pack the cabbage into 2 pint-size jars. Add 2 slices of ginger to each jar and push the vegetables down as far as they will go. Divide the pickling brine between the 2 jars. Place a weight (see page 14 for options) on top of the cabbage to keep it submerged in the brine. Steep for at least 2 days, preferably 5. This pickle keeps for 3 to 4 months in the refrigerator.

INGREDIENT TIP: Chinese mustard cabbage (called gai choy) is a green leafy vegetable from the brassica family. Like all mustards, it's bitter, but when pickled, it mellows in flavor and retains its crunch. Mustard cabbage is readily available at Asian markets.

PINEAPPLE AND CUCUMBER RELISH | ACAR NENAS DAN TIMUN

MALAYSIA

Makes: 1 quart | Prep time: 15 minutes | Curing time: 10 minutes to 1 hour

4 cups fresh pineapple,
   cut into ½-inch cubes
   (½ medium pineapple)
1½ cups cucumber,
   seeded and chopped
   (1 medium cucumber)
1 teaspoon coarse sea
   salt, divided
2 tablespoons rice vinegar
2 tablespoons fresh lime juice
1 tablespoon palm sugar or
   light brown sugar
¼ cup sliced shallots
   (2 small shallots)
1 Thai red chile, chopped

Pineapple's tropical flavor shines in this quick and simple relish called *acar* in Malay. The sweet-tart combination with the addition of cooling cucumber makes for a wonderful complement to curries and barbecued meats hot off the grill. Serve acar cold or at room temperature.

1. Toss the pineapple and cucumber with ½ teaspoon of salt in a colander. Let it sit in the sink while you make the dressing.

2. In a medium bowl, whisk together the vinegar, lime juice, remaining ½ teaspoon of salt, and sugar until the salt and sugar dissolve completely.

3. Drain the pineapple and cucumber and add them to the bowl with the dressing. Add the shallots and chile and toss.

4. Let sit at room temperature for 10 minutes, preferably 1 hour, to allow the flavors to meld. This pickle will keep in the refrigerator for up to 4 days.

INGREDIENT TIP: Palm sugar is sold in discs at Asian markets. To use it in recipes, shave off pieces with a sharp knife. Granulated coconut palm sugar, which is very similar and therefore a good substitute, is available at just about any grocery store.

INDONESIAN FRUIT SALAD | ASINAN BUAH

INDONESIA

Makes: 5 cups | **Prep time:** 15 minutes | **Curing time:** 2 hours

1½ cups underripe mango,
  cut into 1-inch chunks
  (1 medium mango)
1½ cups pineapple, cut into
  1-inch chunks (9 ounces)
1½ cups jicama, cut into
  1-inch chunks (6 ounces)
1 tablespoon palm sugar or
  light brown sugar
1 to 2 teaspoons bottled chile
  paste (or more, depending on
  your taste)
¼ teaspoon fine sea salt
½ cup boiling water
2 tablespoons distilled
  white vinegar

I've always enjoyed asinan buah as a refreshing snack on a hot, sunny day. My mom used to toss in all manner of tropical fruit and vegetables: pineapple, jicama, green mango, star fruit, rose apple, and more. It's also tasty served alongside grilled meats.

1. Drain the mango, pineapple, and jicama in a colander in the sink while you prepare the dressing.

2. In a large heatproof bowl, combine the sugar, chile paste, and salt. Pour in the boiling water and vinegar and stir until the sugar and salt dissolve completely. Taste and adjust the seasonings if desired. Let the dressing cool.

3. Add the fruit to the bowl and toss with the dressing. Refrigerate for at least 2 hours to allow the flavors to meld. Serve chilled or at room temperature. This will keep in the refrigerator for 2 days.

SWITCH THINGS UP: The sweet-sour-spicy dressing is a great way to elevate bland or sour-tasting fruit. When in season, I have used underripe stone fruit like peaches or apricots. But any firm fruit with a tart edge to it or that isn't super sweet would taste great, too.

SOY-PICKLED MUSHROOMS

JAPAN
Makes: 2 cups | Prep and Cook time: 5 minutes | Curing time: 1 hour

⅓ cup soy sauce

⅓ cup rice vinegar

⅔ cup water

¼ cup granulated sugar

8 ounces shiitake mushrooms, stemmed and sliced

Pickling in soy sauce is one of the most basic Japanese pickling techniques. Soy sauce, rice vinegar, and sugar are mixed together to form the brine. Add-ins like mirin, garlic, or chiles are optional. I like to make this tasty side dish with Japanese mini mushrooms like enoki or shimeji (beech mushrooms), but for this recipe, I've used the easier-to-find shiitake. Feel free to use any type of mushroom you can get your hands on, from button to chanterelles.

1. In a small saucepan over medium-high heat, combine the soy sauce, vinegar, water, and sugar and bring to a simmer. Add the mushrooms and cook, stirring occasionally, until the sugar dissolves completely, 3 to 5 minutes.

2. Transfer the mushrooms to a medium bowl with a slotted spoon. Let the brine cool, then pour over the mushrooms. Cover and refrigerate for at least 1 hour. These will keep for up to 2 weeks in the refrigerator.

   TRY IT WITH: These mushrooms are a delicious and nutritious addition to noodle or rice bowls or tossed into a salad.

TURMERIC-SPICED PICKLES | ACAR KUNING

INDONESIA
Makes: 1 quart | Prep time: 25 minutes | Cook time: 5 minutes | Curing time: 12 hours

FOR THE VEGETABLES
½ pound seedless cucumbers,
  like Kirby or Persian,
  cut into matchsticks
  (4 small cucumbers)
½ pound carrots, peeled
  and cut into matchsticks
  (2 medium carrots)
1 teaspoon fine sea salt
1 cup cauliflower florets
¼ cup chopped green
  bell pepper
¼ cup chopped red
  bell pepper
4 Thai red chiles, chopped
2 salam leaves (optional, see
  the ingredient tip)
2 (¼-inch-thick) slices fresh
  galangal, bruised (optional,
  see the ingredient tip)

FOR THE DRESSING
1 cup coarsely chopped shallot
  or red onion
3 candlenuts or macadamia
  nuts, crushed (optional, see
  the ingredient tip)
2 garlic cloves
1 plump stalk lemongrass,
  trimmed and coarsely
  chopped (or 2 tablespoons
  thawed frozen
  ground lemongrass)

In Indonesia, *acar* (pronounced ah-char) is the generic term for pickle and is probably a localized version of Indian achaar. This delicious pickle is literally called "yellow pickle" (after its turmeric-tinged golden hue) and is often eaten with rice and used as a topping for fried fish in the dish ikan acar kuning. For more information on lemongrass, check out the tip in the Lemongrass Chile Sauce recipe (page 78).

1. PREP THE VEGETABLES: Toss the cucumbers and carrots with the salt in a colander. Let them sit to drain in the sink while you make the dressing.

2. MAKE THE DRESSING: Combine the shallots, candlenuts (if using), garlic, and lemongrass in a food processor and whirl until finely chopped to confetti-size bits.

3. Preheat a medium skillet over medium heat. Swirl in the oil. Add the shallot mixture and turmeric. Stir and cook until the paste turns a few shades darker, 2 to 3 minutes.

4. Add the water, vinegar, sugar, and salt. Mix well. Taste and adjust the seasonings if desired. Remove from the heat and let cool for 10 to 15 minutes.

5. PICKLE THE VEGETABLES: When the dressing has cooled, rinse the cucumbers and carrots. Drain and pat dry with paper towels. Add them to the skillet with the dressing, along with the cauliflower, green pepper, red pepper, chiles, salam leaves (if using), and galangal (if using). Mix well. Add ¼ to ½ cup more water if there isn't enough dressing to lightly coat all the vegetables.

6. Transfer the pickles to an airtight container. Cover and let sit in the refrigerator for at least 12 hours to allow the flavors to meld. When ready to serve, remove the salam leaves and galangal. Serve at room temperature with rice or warm over fried fish. This pickle keeps in the refrigerator for 5 days.

INGREDIENT TIP: Salam leaves, galangal, and candlenuts are very typical ingredients used in Indonesian cooking, yet they may be hard to find, even at Asian markets. The candlenuts act as a thickening agent, so macadamias make a decent substitute. If available, salam leaves (also called Indian bay leaves) are usually sold dried in clear cellophane packages. Galangal is available fresh and dried. Soak dried galangal for at least 10 minutes before using in any recipe. These two ingredients have no close substitutes, so omit them if you can't find them.

1 tablespoon vegetable oil

1 teaspoon ground turmeric

½ cup water

2 tablespoons distilled white vinegar

2 tablespoons sugar

1 teaspoon fine sea salt

SWEET AND SPICY PICKLED BABY EGGPLANT

VIETNAM

Makes: 1 quart | Prep and Cook time: 15 minutes, plus 1 hour sitting time | Curing time: 2 days

1 pound baby eggplant (such as Thai, Indian, or fairy tale)

1 teaspoon coarse sea salt or kosher salt

1 cup distilled white vinegar

1 cup water

¼ cup sugar

¼ cup sliced shallot

4 Thai red chiles, sliced or split lengthwise

2 garlic cloves

2 (¼-inch-thick) fresh ginger slices

2 tablespoons fish sauce

Pickled golf-ball-size white eggplants are a Vietnamese favorite. You'll find shelves of them in jars at many Asian markets. They retain their crunch while absorbing all of the delicious sweet, sour, and spicy flavors of this brine. White baby eggplants are not common in the United States, so I've substituted Thai or Indian eggplants, which are about the same size. You can always cut larger eggplants into smaller pieces for the same effect.

1. Stem the eggplants and cut into halves or quarters. Toss with the salt in a large bowl and set aside for 1 hour.

2. Meanwhile, in a small saucepan over medium-high heat, combine the vinegar, water, sugar, shallot, chiles, garlic, and ginger and bring to a boil. Stir until the sugar completely dissolves. Remove from the heat and stir in the fish sauce.

3. Rinse the eggplant under cold running water and drain. Pack into a quart-size jar. Pour the brine over the eggplant and place a weight on top (see page 14 for options) to keep the eggplant submerged under the brine. Seal and steep for at least 2 days in the refrigerator. This pickle keeps for 3 to 4 months in the refrigerator.

SWITCH THINGS UP: This pickle isn't fermented or canned, so you can easily adjust the amounts of sugar and fish sauce to your taste.

MUM'S MIXED PICKLE | ACAR CAMPUR

INDONESIA

Makes: 2 quarts | **Prep and Cook time:** 30 minutes | **Curing time:** 1 to 12 hours

2 pounds seedless cucumbers, like Kirby or Persian, cut into bite-size pieces (12 to 15 cucumbers)

4 ounces cabbage, cut into 1-inch squares (¼ small cabbage)

¾ cup diced red or yellow bell pepper (1 small pepper)

2 cups shredded carrot (8 ounces)

1 cup cauliflower florets (12 ounces)

¼ cup sliced shallot (1½ ounces)

1½ cups distilled white vinegar

¾ cup water

1½ cups sugar

2 tablespoons coarse sea salt or kosher salt

When my mum makes pickles, she makes them with whatever vegetables she has on hand. For some reason, she can't seem to make small amounts and always has more than enough to give away to friends and neighbors. (Don't worry, I have scaled down the quantity of vegetables for this recipe.) And in true Javanese style, she makes them sweet-sweet. You can, of course, reduce the amounts of sugar and salt.

1. In a large bowl, toss the cucumbers, cabbage, bell pepper, carrots, cauliflower, and shallot together.

2. In a medium saucepan over medium heat, combine the vinegar, water, sugar, and salt and bring to a simmer. Stir until the sugar and salt dissolve completely. Taste and adjust the seasonings if desired. Remove from the heat and let cool.

3. Once the brine has cooled down, pour over the vegetables and mix well. Cover and refrigerate for at least 1 hour, preferably 12 hours. These will keep in the refrigerator for 2 to 3 months.

YES YOU CAN! While it's not traditional, this pickle can be canned so it keeps for up to 1 year on the shelf. Double the quantities and follow the canning instructions on page 15. Pack the vegetables into 4 pint-size jars that have been washed with hot, soapy water. Fill the jars with hot brine, leaving a ½-inch headspace. Remove any air bubbles, wipe the rims, and seal the jars. Process in a water-bath canner for 10 minutes. Wait 5 minutes before removing the jars, and check the seals after 12 to 24 hours.

SPICY SMACKED CUCUMBERS | SUAN LA PAI HUANG GUA

CHINA

Makes: 2 cups | **Prep time:** 10 minutes, plus 30 minutes salting time

1 pound thin-skinned cucumber, like English or Persian (1 large or 6 to 8 small cucumbers)

1 tablespoon granulated sugar, plus ¼ teaspoon

1¼ teaspoons coarse sea salt, divided

2 tablespoons rice vinegar

2 teaspoons sesame oil

2 teaspoons chili bean sauce or chili oil

2 large garlic cloves, minced

Toasted sesame seeds, for garnish

Smashed (or smacked) cucumbers are a cool, refreshing "cold dish" that is the perfect foil for rich, spicy food. Smashing the cucumber releases moisture and creates nooks and crannies that allow the cucumber to absorb the dressing readily, making this dish ready in no time. A Chinese cleaver, with its wide, rectangular blade, is the ideal tool for smashing cucumbers, but a large chef's knife or meat pounder will work just as well.

1. Halve each cucumber crosswise, then cut each half lengthwise into four batons. If using small cucumbers, just cut lengthwise into four pieces. Place a piece of cucumber cut-side down on a cutting board. Lay a large knife flat on the cucumber and smash down lightly with your other hand. The skin will split and the seeds will separate from the flesh (discard the seeds, if any). Repeat until all the cucumber pieces are smashed. Cut into bite-size pieces.

2. In a large bowl, toss the cucumber pieces with ¼ teaspoon of sugar and ¼ teaspoon of salt. Place a weight on top of the cucumbers (a smaller bowl or bag filled with ice would work) and set aside for 30 minutes at room temperature or up to 4 hours in the refrigerator.

3. Meanwhile, in a small bowl, stir together the remaining 1 tablespoon of sugar, the remaining 1 teaspoon of salt, and the vinegar until the salt and sugar dissolve. Stir in the sesame oil, chili bean sauce, and garlic.

4. When ready to serve, drain the cucumbers and transfer to a serving bowl. Add the dressing and toss until the cucumbers are well coated. Sprinkle with the sesame seeds and serve immediately. These will last for 2 days in the refrigerator.

SWITCH IT UP: You can use other cucumber varieties, too. Just peel the skin if it's thicker. The smashing technique removes the seeds, so don't worry about removing them.

SLICED PAPAYA PICKLES

VIETNAM

Makes: 1 pint | Prep and Cook time: 10 minutes, plus 10 to 15 minutes salting time |
Curing time: 12 hours to 2 days

1 pound firm green papaya
    (about ½ small papaya)
1 teaspoon coarse sea salt or
    kosher salt
¾ cup rice vinegar
¼ cup water
½ cup sugar
1 Thai red chile, seeded
    and split
2 garlic cloves, smashed

Papaya is so ubiquitous in Southeast Asia that it is eaten as a fruit when fully ripe and as a vegetable when still green and crisp. This pickle uses unripe green papaya, which is sold only at Asian markets. Green papaya looks exactly like regular papaya but will have a uniformly green peel. You will usually find it in the produce section next to the taro and sweet potatoes. Don't know what to do with the second half of the papaya? Use it as if it were zucchini.

1. Halve the papaya lengthwise. Remove the seeds with a spoon. Reserve one half for another use—stored in a plastic bag in the refrigerator, it will keep for 2 weeks. Peel the papaya with a peeler and rinse well. Place cut-side down on a cutting board. Cut crosswise into ⅛-inch-thick slices with a very sharp knife, or use a mandoline if you have one. In a medium bowl, toss the papaya slices with the salt and set aside until soft and pliable, 10 to 15 minutes.

2. Meanwhile, in a small saucepan, combine the rice vinegar, water, and sugar. Bring to a boil over medium-high heat, stirring until the sugar dissolves completely. Set aside to cool.

3. Rinse and drain the papaya and pack into a pint-size jar. Add the red chile and garlic. Pour the brine into the jar, making sure to submerge the papaya slices. Seal and refrigerate for at least 12 hours or up to 2 days. The papaya is ready when it turns translucent. It will keep for up to 1 month in the refrigerator.

    INGREDIENT TIP: If you can't find green papaya, look for a moderately ripe papaya that's yellowish but still firm. Kohlrabi also makes an excellent substitute.

SESAME ZUCCHINI THREADS | HOBAK NAMUL

KOREA

Makes: 2 cups | **Prep time:** 1 hour, plus 15 minutes salting time | **Curing time:** 5 minutes

20 ounces zucchini
  (4 medium zucchini)
5 ounces carrot
  (1 medium carrot)
1 Korean green chile or
  jalapeño (optional)
1 teaspoon fine sea salt
2 tablespoons fresh lemon
  juice (from ½ large lemon)
1 tablespoon sesame oil
½ teaspoon grated fresh
  ginger (from a 1-inch piece)
2 teaspoons granulated sugar
Dash ground white pepper
1 teaspoon toasted sesame
  seeds, for garnish

This dish is not a pickle per se but more of a seasoned vegetable dish. Colorful and elegant, it has a gentle and mild flavor that is especially calming with spicy food. An assortment of similar dishes is typically served as banchan, or small side dishes, during a traditional Korean meal.

1. Halve the zucchini lengthwise and scrape out the seeds with a spoon. Using a very sharp paring knife or julienne peeler, cut the zucchini as thinly as possible into long threads. Cut the carrot and green chile (if using) to the same size as the zucchini.

2. Toss the zucchini and carrot with the salt in a colander and let the mixture drain in the sink for 15 minutes. Wrap the vegetables in a non-terry-cloth dish towel and gently wring out excess moisture. Do this two or three times to extract the moisture from the vegetables, but don't completely crush them. They should be somewhat dry to the touch.

3. Put the zucchini and carrot in a medium bowl and fluff them up. Add the lemon juice, chile (if using), sesame oil, ginger, sugar, and pepper. Let sit for 5 minutes to allow the flavors to meld. Just before serving, sprinkle with the sesame seeds. Toss and serve. This will keep for up to 5 days in the refrigerator.

PREP TIP: This dish can be made a few hours ahead, but wait until just before serving to drizzle the sesame oil over the top.

PICKLED GINGER | GARI

JAPAN

Makes: 1 pint | **Prep and Cook time:** 15 minutes, plus 10 minutes soaking time | **Curing time:** 12 hours

4 ounces young ginger

1 teaspoon coarse sea salt or kosher salt, divided

¼ cup rice vinegar

¼ cup water

2 tablespoons granulated sugar

Japanese pickled ginger, or gari, is best known as the palate cleanser eaten with sushi or sashimi. With its mild flavor and tender texture, young ginger is best for making gari. Young ginger also has pink tips, which naturally color the gari. Commercially produced pickled ginger is often artificially dyed pink. Find young ginger at specialty markets like Whole Foods or at a farmers' market. It's definitely worth your while to make gari at home, as it won't contain dyes and the flavor will be more delicate.

1. Separate the ginger into manageable knobs, 1 to 2 inches long. Gently scrape the skin from each knob with a teaspoon. Cut the ginger into very thin slices (about 1/16-inch thick) along the grain. Soak in a bowl of water at room temperature for 10 minutes.

2. Bring a small pot of water to a boil over medium-high heat. Add the ginger and bring the water back to a boil. Simmer for 1 minute and remove from the heat.

3. Drain the water from the pot and sprinkle ½ teaspoon of salt over the ginger while still hot.

4. Once the ginger is cool enough to handle, massage for 1 minute. Squeeze out as much liquid as possible and pack into a pint-size jar.

5. In the small pot, combine the vinegar, water, sugar, and remaining ½ teaspoon of salt and bring to a boil over medium heat. Stir until the sugar dissolves completely. Taste and adjust the seasonings if desired. Remove from the heat and set aside to cool.

6. Pour the brine over the ginger. Seal and keep in a cool dark place for 12 hours. This pickle will keep in the refrigerator for up to 6 months.

INGREDIENT TIP: If you can't find young ginger, look for a fresh hand of ginger that is smooth with shiny, taut skin. The skin should be thin and not thick and fibrous. You will have to boil mature ginger for longer—around 3 minutes—to remove its spiciness in step 2. I would also allow it to pickle for longer.

PICKLED BEAN SPROUTS | DƯA GIÁ

VIETNAM

Makes: 4 cups | Prep and Cook time: 10 minutes | Curing time: 1 hour

1½ cups water

½ cup distilled white vinegar

½ cup granulated sugar

1 teaspoon coarse sea salt or kosher salt

Freshly ground black pepper

8 ounces mung bean sprouts, rinsed under cool water

1 small carrot, shredded

1 small bunch Chinese chives or skinny green onions, cut into 2-inch pieces

1 red Fresno or serrano chile, seeded and sliced

This refreshing pickle has a satisfying crunch and contrasts nicely with the rich and robust flavors of Vietnamese dishes like caramelized pork belly and eggs or caramelized catfish in a clay pot. It would even be just as tasty in a banh mi sandwich. The bean sprouts provide the crunch, but the distinct aroma comes from the Chinese chives, which have flatter leaves and a more pungent taste than the chives at the grocery store. Try to find them, but if you can't, green onions will work fine, too.

1. In a small saucepan over medium heat, combine the water, vinegar, sugar, and salt and bring to a simmer. Stir until the sugar and salt dissolve completely. Add a few grinds of black pepper. Set aside to cool.

2. In a large bowl, toss together the bean sprouts, carrot, chives, and chile slices. Pour the brine over the vegetables. Don't worry if the vegetables aren't completely submerged. They will shrink in volume, allowing the brine to completely cover them. Set aside at room temperature for at least 1 hour, tossing occasionally.

3. To serve, use tongs or a slotted spoon to scoop up the vegetables, leaving the brine behind. Refrigerate any leftovers. This pickle is best eaten within 2 to 3 days, or the bean sprouts will lose their crunch.

SWITCH IT UP: If you can't find mung bean sprouts, try pickling soybean sprouts or sunflower sprouts. Just don't use alfalfa sprouts—they are too fragile.

SESAME PICKLED CABBAGE

JAPAN

Makes: 1 quart | **Prep time:** 15 minutes

1 pound green cabbage

1½ teaspoons coarse sea salt or kosher salt

1 tablespoon sesame oil

1 tablespoon toasted sesame seeds, for garnish

Salting and massaging vegetables is one of the easiest Japanese techniques for pickling. All you have to do is combine the vegetables—in this case, cabbage—with salt in a zip-top bag and massage the salt into them. Plus, it is ready in no time. Adding the sesame oil elevates an otherwise bland pickle while adding a distinctive aroma.

1. Core the cabbage and coarsely chop the leaves into 2-by-2-inch squares.

2. Put the cabbage and salt in a zip-top bag. Seal the bag with air inside and shake to distribute the salt evenly. Massage the cabbage until it is soft and has released its juices, about 5 minutes. Drain the liquid.

3. Add the sesame oil to the bag and massage into the cabbage. Transfer the cabbage to a serving plate and sprinkle with the sesame seeds. Toss and serve. This will keep in the refrigerator for 3 days.

SWITCH IT UP: This recipe works well with vegetables aside from cabbage, including turnips and daikon radish.

PICKLED GREEN CHILES

SINGAPORE

Makes: 1½ cups | Prep time: 10 minutes | Curing time: 12 hours

4 ounces mild green chiles, like serrano or jalapeño, seeded and sliced (4 to 6 chiles)

1 cup rice vinegar

1 cup hot water

1 teaspoon salt

½ teaspoon sugar

Growing up in Singapore, I always had a little dish of pickled green chiles doused in soy sauce to accompany wonton noodles. Even though I've always been spice-averse, this is one chile pickle that I can tolerate, because the vinegar mellows the chiles' spiciness, leaving my taste buds to enjoy the nice crunch and tang.

1. Bring a kettle of water to a boil. Place the chiles in a small bowl. Pour boiling water over the chiles and blanch for 10 seconds. Drain and discard the water.

2. Pack the chiles into a quart-size jar.

3. In a small heatproof bowl, combine the vinegar, hot water, salt, and sugar. Stir until the salt and sugar dissolve completely. Set aside to cool.

4. Pour the brine into the jar. Seal and refrigerate for 12 hours. Pickled green chiles keep in the refrigerator for up to 2 months.

TRY IT WITH: Pickled green chiles can be served with soy sauce to accompany any noodle dish. Don't hesitate to try them on pizza and in sandwiches, too.

SPICY PICKLED LOTUS ROOT

JAPAN

Makes: 1 pint | Prep and Cook time: 10 minutes | Curing time: 12 hours

6 to 8 ounces lotus root, peeled and cut into thin rounds (1 small lotus root)

2 tablespoons rice vinegar

1 tablespoon sugar

2 teaspoons soy sauce

¼ teaspoon coarse sea salt or kosher salt

2 teaspoons sesame oil

1 teaspoon chili oil

1 small dried red chile, like chile de arbol, crushed

Lotus root has long been prized in Asian cultures for its health benefits. It is low in calories, is high in dietary fiber, and contains many vitamins and minerals, including vitamin B, vitamin C, iron, potassium, copper, thiamin, and zinc. Its mild flavor and crunchy texture make it an excellent vehicle for pickling.

1. Rinse the lotus root in water.

2. Bring a medium saucepan of water to a boil over medium-high heat and add the lotus root. When the water returns to a boil, simmer for 1 minute. Drain and place the lotus root in a container with a lid.

3. In a small bowl, stir together the rice vinegar, sugar, soy sauce, salt, sesame oil, chili oil, and dried chile. Pour over the lotus root and toss to mix. Cover the container and refrigerate for 12 hours. This will keep for 1 month in the refrigerator.

INGREDIENT TIP: Lotus root is actually the rhizome of the lotus flower. They have segments linked like sausages and are usually sold in shorter portions. Find them in the produce section at Asian markets. If you have trouble finding lotus root, jicama or water chestnuts are good substitutes.

SALT-PICKLED VEGETABLES | SHIOZUKE

JAPAN

Makes: 1 quart | Prep time: 10 minutes | Curing time: 2 to 8 hours

3 mini seedless cucumbers,
   like Kirby or Persian
2 small carrots
10 ounces daikon radish
   (1 small radish)
¼ cup coarse sea salt or
   kosher salt
4 cups warm water
Optional mix-ins: garlic
   (1 clove), ginger (2 thin
   slices), kombu (1-inch
   square piece), chiles
   (1 to 2 peppers), citrus zest
   (2-inch piece)

Shiozuke is a Japanese tsukemono (which means "pickled things") made with just salt and vegetables. I use a salt-to-water ratio of 1 tablespoon salt to 1 cup water, but the amount of salt and the pickling time can be altered to suit your preferences. Here, I have chosen to pickle cucumbers, carrots, and daikon, but feel free to use any vegetable in season. Keep in mind that the size and texture of your vegetables will determine how quickly the pickles will reach your desired level of saltiness. If you cut the vegetables to create more surface area, the pickling process is faster than if you leave the vegetables whole, halved, or quartered. Experiment to determine your favorite combinations.

1. Peel the cucumbers in alternating ½-inch-wide strips. Peel the carrots. Peel the daikon and cut crosswise to the same length as the cucumber and carrot. Then cut all the vegetables into halves or quarters, depending on their size. Place the vegetables in one or more containers or zip-top bags large enough to hold them, the brine, and a weight. You can choose to use one to three separate containers. I use rectangular Pyrex glass containers with tight-fitting lids.

2. Stir the salt into the warm water until it dissolves completely. Add any optional mix-ins if desired. When the brine is cool, pour it over the vegetables to completely cover them. Save any leftover brine in the refrigerator. Place a weight (see page 14 for options) on top to keep the vegetables submerged under the brine. Refrigerate for a minimum of 2 hours and no longer than 8 hours.

3. Drain the vegetables and save the brine to pickle more. Wrap the vegetables in paper towels to absorb all liquid. Cut the vegetables you will serve immediately on the bias into bite-size pieces and arrange on a plate. Serve.

4. Leave the remaining pickled vegetables uncut. They will keep in the refrigerator for 3 to 4 days.

TRY IT WITH: This dish is a perfect accompaniment to a meal of rice, miso soup, and a protein. Salt-pickling vegetables makes it easy to have vegetables with every meal. They also make for a tasty and healthy snack.

SHREDDED VEGETABLE PICKLES | ACHARA

PHILIPPINES

Makes: 2 pints | **Prep and Cook time:** 30 minutes, plus 1 hour salting time | **Curing time:** 12 hours

1 pound firm green papaya, peeled and shredded (½ small papaya)

1 pound jicama, peeled and shredded (1 medium jicama)

1 cup peeled and shredded carrot (1 medium carrot)

1 cup sliced red bell pepper (1 small pepper)

1 cup thinly sliced red onion (1 small onion)

3 tablespoons coarse sea salt or kosher salt, divided

3 cups rice vinegar

1 cup water

1½ cups sugar

3 garlic cloves, smashed

1 (2-inch) knob fresh ginger, peeled and cut into matchsticks

1 fresh red chile, like Fresno or serrano, thinly sliced (optional)

Freshly ground black pepper

Achara is the catchall term for Filipino-style pickles, generally made with souring agents that range from vinegar to lime juice to tamarind. The main ingredient is usually green papaya, but I like to add some jicama as well. You can also add radishes or kohlrabi to the mix. Enjoy achara as you would a relish or salsa, to add texture and tang to grilled meats or fish.

1. Toss the papaya, jicama, carrot, bell pepper, and onion with 2 tablespoons of salt in a colander. Place a weight on top and set aside to drain in the sink for 1 hour.

2. Meanwhile, in a medium saucepan over medium-high heat, combine the vinegar, water, sugar, remaining 1 tablespoon of salt, garlic, ginger, and chile (if using). Bring to a boil and stir until the sugar and salt dissolve completely. Reduce the heat to medium-low and simmer for 15 to 20 minutes to allow the flavors to meld. Remove from the heat and add a few grinds of black pepper.

3. Rinse the vegetables under cold running water. Wrap handfuls of vegetables in a non-terry-cloth dish towel or cheesecloth and squeeze to remove excess moisture. You may need to do this in several batches.

4. Pack the vegetables into 2 pint-size jars and pour enough of the pickling solution over each to cover the vegetables by ¼ inch. Seal and keep in the refrigerator for at least 12 hours, then serve at room temperature. Achara keeps for up to 6 months in the refrigerator.

INGREDIENT TIP: To make light work of shredding the vegetables, use a mandoline, box shredder, julienne peeler, or a Vietnamese slicer and shredder tool called dao bao. You can also use the shredding attachment tool on a food processor. The size of the shreds makes no difference, as long as the vegetables are all of similar size.

INDONESIAN CHILI PASTE | SAMBAL OELEK, PAGE 57

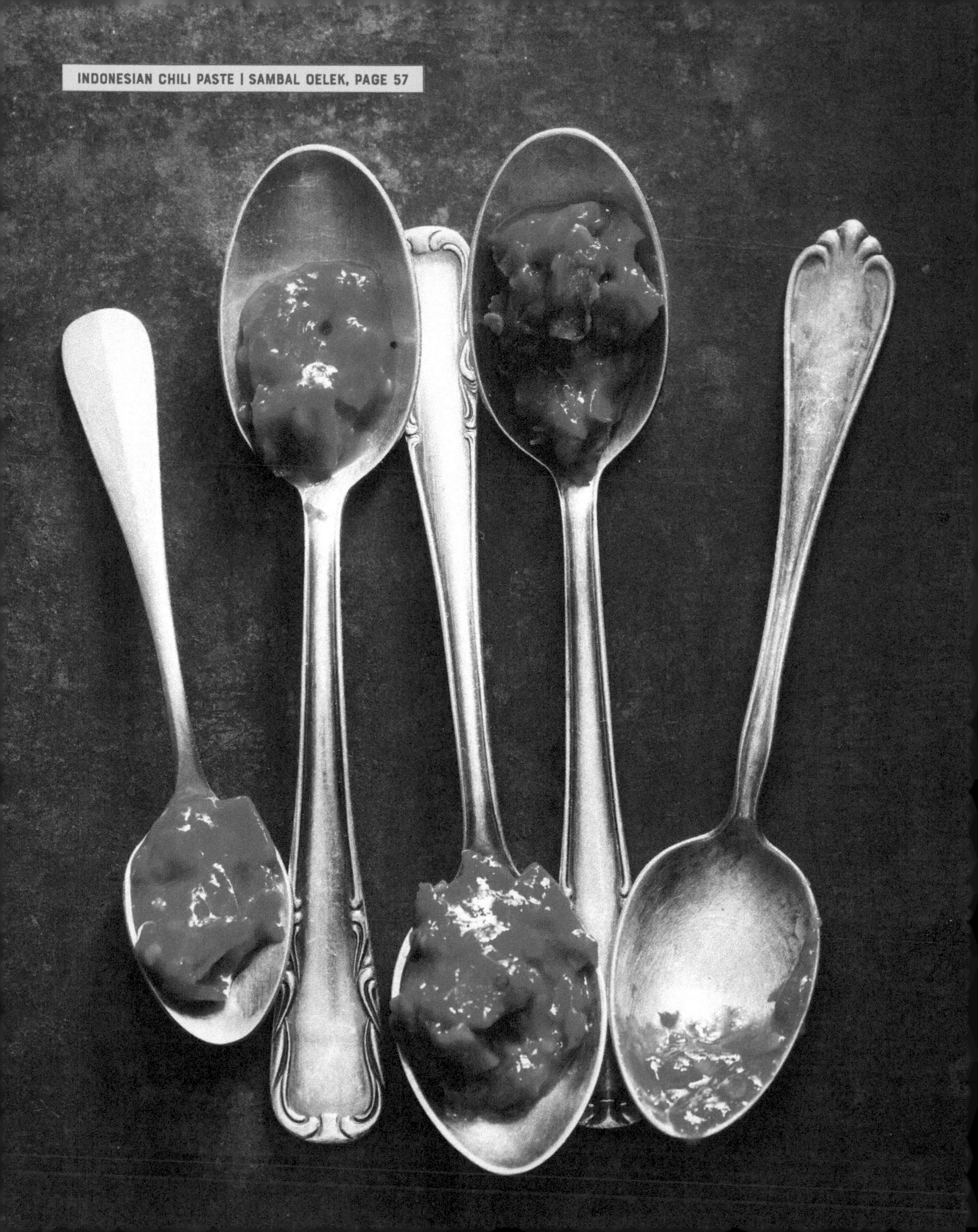

CHAPTER 3

Chutneys, Sauces, and Seasonings

Roasted Chile Jam | Nam Prik Pao 56

Indonesian Chile Paste | Sambal Oelek 57

Shrimp Paste Sambal | Sambal Terasi 58

Lime Juice Pickle 60

Thai Sweet Chile Sauce 62

Mango Chutney 63

Tomato-Date Chutney 64

Cilantro-Mint Chutney 65

Green Mango Pickle 66

Sweet, Sour, and Spicy Mango Sauce | Amba 68

Fiery Lime Pickle | Nimbu Ka Achaar 70

Sri Lankan Chile Paste | Katta Sambol 72

Plum Sauce (or Duck Sauce) 73

Banana Ketchup 74

Fermented White Tofu | Bai Fu Ru 76

Lemongrass Chile Sauce 78

Momo Sauce 79

Korean Red Pepper Paste | Gochujang 80

PICKLE PASSPORT: INDIA

*Must-try pickles: Fiery Lime Pickle (page 70), Green Mango Pickle (page 66),
Mango Chutney (page 63), Sweet, Sour, and Spicy Mango Sauce (page 68)*

Pickling goes way back in India. In fact, the Museum of Food and
Drink in New York City reports that cucumbers native to India were
first pickled in 2030 BCE in the Tigris Valley. As in many places,
pickling started in India as a way to preserve foods for travel and
for long periods.

There are two basic types of Indian pickles: pickles that are
preserved in oil and pickles that are not. Pickles preserved in oil
are widely considered *the* Indian pickle. Collectively known as
achaar or aachar in Hindi, these pickles are quite different from
the Western idea of a pickle. Yes, various kinds of produce are
pickled with salt (and sometimes sugar), but the crowning touch
is a tadka, made by tempering spices in oil. This seasoning oil is
typically redolent with fenugreek seeds, mustard seeds, and curry
leaves, and it is folded into the pickle, where it acts as a preservative. The type of oil favored depends on region. Southern states
prefer sesame oil. In the north, mustard oil is used extensively
for cooking and particularly in achaars. Mustard oil is prized for
its spicy, wasabi-like aroma, but its use is restricted in the United
States, because it contains high levels of erucic acid that may
contribute to the development of heart disease. You can still find
mustard oil at Indian markets, but it is labeled "for external use
only." While millions of people consume it in India regularly, you
should use mustard oil at your own discretion.

A traditional Indian meal is not complete without achaar. In fact, a basic meal may comprise just achaar and rice. Achaar may complement biryanis, curries, and tandoori meats. Achaars can be made from a variety of fruits and vegetables: limes, eggplant, cauliflower, and carrots. Fish and meats are also pickled. Mangos, however, are at the top of the totem pole. Mango achaar is usually made during the summer months, when the fruit is abundant.

Mangos also show up in chutneys. Technically more of a relish than a pickle, chutneys are made by combining fruit, herbs, and/or vegetables with a souring agent. True Indian chutneys are savory, like Cilantro-Mint Chutney (page 65), coconut chutney, and peanut chutney. Sweet fruit chutneys made with fruit, vinegar, and sugar, like Mango Chutney (page 63) and plum chutney, are probably an Anglo-Indian invention that originated during British rule in India, between 1858 and 1947.

ROASTED CHILE JAM | NAM PRIK PAO

THAILAND

Makes: 1½ cups | Prep time: 10 minutes | Cook time: 20 minutes

6 ounces fresh long red chiles,
 like Fresno or serrano, seeded
 if desired (8 chiles)

2 Thai red chiles (optional)

½ to 1 cup vegetable oil,
 like canola, divided and
 as needed

2 small heads garlic, peeled
 (16 cloves)

3 ounces small shallots or
 pickling red onions, peeled
 (6 to 8 shallots)

¼ cup palm sugar or light
 brown sugar

2 tablespoons lime juice

2 tablespoons fish sauce

½ cup water

This dark, flavorful chile paste often accompanies the popular Thai red curry noodle dish khao soi. The original recipe calls for shrimp paste and dried shrimp, but I've omitted them to simplify it. Not to worry, though: The fish sauce still adds umami, and frying the paste in the last step deepens the flavor.

1. In a large dry skillet over medium heat, roast all of the chiles for 6 to 8 minutes, turning occasionally, until they are lightly charred. Transfer to a plate and set aside to cool.

2. In the same skillet over medium heat, heat ½ cup of oil until shimmering hot. Fry the garlic and shallots, turning frequently, until they are golden brown on the outside and soft inside, 8 to 10 minutes. Set aside to cool.

3. When the chiles are cool enough to handle, peel off any burnt spots. Put the chiles in the bowl of a small food processor and blitz until they resemble confetti. Add the garlic and shallots and blitz until a coarse paste forms.

4. Add more oil to the skillet—about ½ cup—and heat over medium heat. Stir in the chile paste, sugar, lime juice, fish sauce, and water. Stir and cook over medium heat until the mixture turns into a thick, dark, aromatic paste, about 10 minutes. Remove from the heat and set aside to cool completely. Once it is cool, use immediately or store in a sealed glass jar in the refrigerator for up to 2 weeks.

TRY IT WITH: Use this chile paste to flavor stir-fries. I like it particularly with okra, but eggplant and zucchini would taste great, too.

INDONESIAN CHILE PASTE | SAMBAL OELEK

INDONESIA
Makes: ¼ cup | Prep time: 10 minutes

2½ ounces fresh long red
   chiles, like Fresno or serrano,
   seeded if desired and
   chopped (2 chiles)
⅛ teaspoon coarse sea salt or
   kosher salt
1 tablespoon fresh lime or Key
   lime juice
Pinch sugar (optional)

The Indonesian word *oelek* means to "to grind," and sambal oelek refers to a chile paste that is ground in a mortar with a pestle. In its simplest form, this chile paste is made from chiles, salt, and lime juice. You can always add some bird or Thai chiles to make it spicier. While you can find sambal oelek in jars, in Indonesia it's always made fresh to order. You'll love how much fresher tasting this quick option is. I like it on fried rice and as a dip for fresh vegetables. If you want to make it in bulk, just multiply the ingredients and use a food processor.

Place the chiles and salt in a mortar. Grind the chiles with the pestle, using a twisting motion, until pulpy. Stir in the lime juice and sugar (if using). Taste and adjust the seasonings if desired. Serve immediately.

SWITCH IT UP: There are dozens of different types of chile paste in Indonesia. Try experimenting by adding ingredients like garlic, shallots, lemongrass, and lime leaves.

INDONESIA

Makes: 1 cup | **Prep time:** 15 minutes | **Cook time:** 5 minutes

1 block dried shrimp paste
(see the ingredient tip)

6 ounces fresh long red chiles,
like Fresno or serrano,
seeded and coarsely chopped
(8 chiles)

1 tablespoon palm sugar or
dark brown sugar

1 tablespoon freshly squeezed
lime or Key lime juice

Shrimp paste sambal comes in two forms: fresh or cooked. This is my super-easy fresh version. The key ingredient in this sambal is dried shrimp paste (terasi/trassi in Indonesian), made by fermenting shrimp and salt for many months in the sun. While terasi has an overpowering odor raw, it mellows dramatically when cooked and adds tons of umami to a dish. There is no substitute for shrimp paste. I use sambal terasi as a dipping sauce for fried chicken and fried eggs or as a flavoring paste for stir-fries.

1. Open a window and turn your fan on full blast.

2. Cut two slices (or as many slices as fit in your pan), each about ¼-inch thick, from the block of shrimp paste. Put the slices in a small dry skillet and toast until browned and fragrant, about 5 minutes. The shrimp paste should no longer be soft on the inside and should crumble easily. Grind the toasted shrimp paste in a mortar with a pestle, or place in a zip-top bag and pound with a meat pounder until a coarse powder forms. Measure out 1 tablespoon and save the remainder for another use (such as in a stir-fry or soup). The paste lasts for 6 months in the refrigerator.

3. In a mortar, combine 1 tablespoon toasted shrimp paste with the chiles, sugar, and lime juice and grind with a pestle. You may have to add the chiles gradually. You may also blitz the mixture in a small food processor until the paste resembles cooked oatmeal. Serve immediately. This sambal keeps for 1 week in the refrigerator.

INGREDIENT TIP: Terasi is sold in 250-gram blocks at Asian markets, or sometimes in small packs of 5 grams each. You may find blocks of shrimp paste labeled "belachan," which is Malay for shrimp paste, and they can be used interchangeably. If you're lucky, you may find granulated shrimp paste that's already toasted, is much easier to use, and allows you to skip the toasting part of step 2.

LIME JUICE PICKLE

INDIA

Makes: ½ cup | **Prep time:** 10 minutes | **Cook time:** 5 minutes | **Fermenting time:** 1 to 4 days

FOR THE PICKLE

1 tablespoon sesame seeds

1 teaspoon fenugreek seeds

½ teaspoon mustard seeds

½ cup fresh lime juice (from 4 large limes)

1 tablespoon ground red chili powder, like cayenne

¼ teaspoon ground turmeric

1 teaspoon coarse sea salt or kosher salt

FOR TEMPERING

2 tablespoons vegetable oil, like canola

¼ teaspoon cumin seeds

¼ teaspoon mustard seeds

¼ teaspoon fenugreek seeds

4 or 5 curry leaves

2 small dried red chiles, like chiles de arbol, crushed

Unlike Fiery Lime Pickle (page 70), this pickle contains only lime juice and no lime pieces. It's a great pickle to make when you've run out of vegetables. It's quick and easy to make, and once you have the spices, it can be made on demand. Fermenting intensifies the flavors, but if you're impatient, skip it. This tangy, spicy condiment brightens up any rice dish and even oatmeal!

1. Wash all your equipment with hot, soapy water.

2. MAKE THE PICKLE MIXTURE: In a small dry skillet over medium heat, toast the sesame, fenugreek, and mustard seeds until they start to pop and release their fragrance, 2 to 3 minutes. Remove from the heat and grind in a spice grinder or with a mortar and pestle.

3. In a small bowl, whisk together the ground spice mixture, lime juice, chili powder, turmeric, and salt until there are no lumps.

4. If you have the time, cover the bowl with cheesecloth and ferment for 1 to 4 days at room temperature.

5. TEMPER THE PICKLE: When ready to serve, heat the oil in a small skillet over medium heat. Add the cumin, mustard, and fenugreek seeds. When the seeds start to pop and release their fragrance, 30 seconds to 1 minute, add the curry leaves and red chiles and stir for about 1 minute. Be careful not to burn the chiles and curry leaves. Remove from the heat and set aside to cool.

6. When the tempering oil is cool, add it to the lime juice mixture. Serve immediately. This pickle keeps for 2 weeks in the refrigerator.

INGREDIENT TIP: Curry leaves are available fresh and sometimes frozen at Indian and Asian markets. If you can't find them, omit them. If possible, buy whole spices and buy only what you need in the bulk section. Spices lose their flavor and aroma about 6 months after purchase. A blade coffee grinder (not a burr grinder) can double as a spice grinder. Just be sure to clean it thoroughly by grinding some uncooked rice inside before and after. This will keep your spices from tasting like coffee and vice versa.

THAI SWEET CHILE SAUCE

THAILAND
Makes: 1 quart | **Prep time:** 15 minutes | **Cook time:** 45 minutes to 1 hour

8 ounces fresh long red chiles, like Fresno or serrano, mostly seeded and coarsely chopped (8 chiles)

6 Thai red chiles, coarsely chopped (optional)

8 garlic cloves, coarsely chopped

¼ teaspoon salt

1½ cups distilled white vinegar

3 cups water

2½ cups sugar

1 (1-inch) knob fresh ginger, peeled and cut into 3 or 4 coins

This sweet chile sauce is so versatile. Use it to flavor stir-fried vegetables or as a dipping sauce for fried spring rolls. You can tinker with the sweet-tart balance toward the end of cooking by adding sugar or vinegar.

1. In the bowl of a food processor or blender, combine both types of chiles, the garlic, and the salt and blitz to confetti-size bits.

2. Transfer the chile mixture to a large nonreactive saucepan. Add the vinegar, water, sugar, and ginger coins and bring to a boil over medium-high heat. Reduce the heat to a simmer and simmer until the volume has reduced by half and the sauce is as thick as syrup. The timing will depend on how wide and deep your pan is. Remove from the heat and set aside to cool completely. The sauce will thicken even further.

3. Remove the ginger coins. Pour the sauce into 4 half-pint jars. Use immediately or refrigerate. This sauce keeps for 6 months in the refrigerator.

   YES YOU CAN! While it's not traditional, this sauce can be canned so it keeps for up to 1 year on the shelf. Following the canning instructions on page 15, pour the hot sauce into 4 half-pint jars that have been washed with soap and hot water, leaving a ½-inch headspace. Remove any air bubbles, wipe the rims, and seal the jars. Process in a water-bath canner for 10 minutes. Wait 5 minutes before removing the jars, and check the seals after 12 to 24 hours.

MANGO CHUTNEY

INDIA
Makes: 1 pint | **Prep time:** 15 minutes | **Cook time:** 45 minutes to 1 hour | **Curing time:** 2 weeks

4 cups green or underripe mangos, peeled and cut into ½-inch cubes (2 large mangos)

2 teaspoons coarse sea salt or kosher salt, divided

1½ cups apple cider vinegar

1 cup sugar

1 tablespoon minced garlic

1 tablespoon grated fresh ginger

¼ cup golden sultanas, raisins, or currants

½ teaspoon ground turmeric

1 fresh long green chile, like jalapeño or serrano, split lengthwise

Mango chutney is a delicious addition to any meal, South Asian or otherwise. It's lovely served with roast chicken or spread on a grilled cheese sandwich. Alternatively, thin it with water to glaze pork tenderloin.

1. In a large nonreactive bowl, toss the mangos with 1 teaspoon of salt and set aside.

2. In a large pot over medium heat, combine the vinegar and sugar and bring to a gentle boil, stirring until the sugar dissolves completely. Add the garlic, ginger, sultanas, turmeric, chile, and remaining 1 teaspoon salt and bring back to a boil.

3. Add the mangos and mix well. Adjust the heat and simmer for 45 minutes to 1 hour, until the mangos turn translucent and the chutney has thickened, stirring occasionally. Taste (it should be mostly sweet with a touch of sour) and adjust the seasonings if desired. Remove from the heat and pick out the chile.

4. Ladle the chutney into 2 half-pint jars, leaving a ½-inch headspace. This chutney can be eaten immediately, but it tastes better after the flavors have melded for at least 2 weeks. It keeps in the refrigerator for up to 1 year.

YES YOU CAN! Mango chutney can be canned so it keeps for up to 1 year on the shelf. Double the quantities. Following the canning instructions on page 15, ladle the hot chutney into 2 hot, pint-size jars that have been washed with hot, soapy water, leaving a ½-inch headspace. Remove any air bubbles, wipe the rims, and seal the jars. Process in a water-bath canner for 10 minutes. Wait 5 minutes before removing the jars, and check the seals after 12 to 24 hours.

TOMATO-DATE CHUTNEY

INDIA

Makes: 2 cups | **Prep time:** 10 minutes | **Cook time:** 15 minutes

2 tablespoons vegetable oil

¼ teaspoon fennel seeds

¼ teaspoon cumin seeds

¼ teaspoon black
  mustard seeds

¼ teaspoon fenugreek seeds

¼ teaspoon nigella seeds

2 small dried red chiles, like
  chiles de arbol, crushed,
  seeded if desired

1 teaspoon grated fresh ginger

½ pound Roma tomatoes (4 or
  5 tomatoes)

½ teaspoon coarse sea salt or
  kosher salt

1 tablespoon raisins

2 tablespoons dates, pitted
  and chopped (4 large dates)

2 teaspoons sugar

1 teaspoon dried mango
  powder (amchur powder,
  see the ingredient tip) or
  lime juice

Tomato-date chutney is a sweet, spicy chutney that is flavored with panch phoron, or Bengali five-spice mix. Panch phoron generally is made of the following five whole spices: fennel seeds, cumin seeds, black mustard seeds, fenugreek seeds, and nigella seeds. Even if you don't have all the spices, the dish will still be very fragrant. This chutney is delicious eaten as an appetizer, as a snack with papadum (thin, crisp flatbread made from black gram flour), or as a side dish with flatbread like chapatti or naan. Try it with another dried fruit (like figs, cherries, or cranberries) if you like.

1. In a large saucepan over medium-high heat, warm the oil. Add the fennel seeds, cumin seeds, mustard seeds, fenugreek seeds, and nigella seeds. Fry until the seeds start to pop and release their fragrance, 2 to 3 minutes. Add the chiles and stir a few seconds. Stir in the ginger and cook until fragrant, 30 seconds to 1 minute.

2. Add the whole tomatoes and salt and stir to combine. Cover and cook over medium-low heat until the tomatoes soften and fall apart, 9 to 10 minutes.

3. Stir in the raisins and dates. Add the sugar and mango powder. Stir often, breaking up the tomatoes into small bits with a wooden spatula or spoon. Cook until the chutney thickens, 4 to 5 minutes. If the chutney starts sticking to the pan, add water 1 tablespoon at a time. Taste and add more sugar or salt if desired. Remove from the heat and serve immediately. Store leftovers in an airtight container in the refrigerator for 4 to 5 days.

INGREDIENT TIP: Mango powder, or amchur, is made by drying green, unripe mango slices in the sun, then grinding them to a fine powder. Like tamarind, it adds a pleasant sweet-sour taste to dishes. You can find it at Indian or Asian grocery stores.

CILANTRO-MINT CHUTNEY

INDIA

Makes: 1 cup | **Prep time:** 10 minutes

3 fresh green chiles, like jalapeño, serrano, or Korean, seeded if desired

½ cup packed cilantro leaves

½ cup packed fresh mint leaves

¼ teaspoon coarse sea salt or kosher salt

¼ teaspoon sugar

2½ teaspoons lemon juice

¼ cup water

¼ teaspoon chaat masala (optional)

1 tablespoon yogurt (optional)

Cilantro-mint chutney is quick and easy to make. In addition to accompanying Indian snacks like samosas and papadum, this chutney is tasty in tacos or as a dip for tortilla chips. With the addition of yogurt, it makes a nice salad dressing or sauce for grilled vegetables. It is also a very versatile green chile sauce. Depending on your preference or mood, you can use all cilantro or all mint. Just add two small cloves of garlic (garlic-mint chutney!) or a 2-inch piece of fresh ginger (ginger-cilantro chutney!).

Combine the chiles, cilantro, mint, salt, sugar, lemon juice, water, and chaat masala (if using) in a food processor or blender. Blitz until a smooth sauce forms. Taste and add more salt and/or lemon juice if desired. If it isn't spicy enough, add more chiles and blitz again. Pour into a serving bowl and stir in the yogurt (if using). Serve immediately. This chutney keeps for up to 5 days in the refrigerator, or you can freeze it in an airtight container for up to 3 months.

INGREDIENT TIP: Chaat masala is a spice mix of dried mango powder, cumin, coriander, ginger, salt, black pepper, asafoetida, and chili powder. It's available at Indian markets.

GREEN MANGO PICKLE

INDIA

Makes: 1 quart | **Prep and Cook time:** 15 minutes, plus 2 hours dehydrating time | **Curing time:** 2 days to 1 week

FOR THE PICKLE

4 to 5 cups green or underripe mangos, unpeeled, roughly chopped (2 large mangos)

2 tablespoons coarse sea salt or kosher salt

2 tablespoons mild red chili powder like Kashmiri (or a mix of paprika and red chili powder for milder palates)

2 teaspoons ground cumin

1 teaspoon ground turmeric

1 teaspoon ground coriander

FOR TEMPERING

¼ cup fenugreek seeds

2 teaspoons black mustard seeds

¼ cup vegetable oil, like canola

4 garlic cloves, minced

2 teaspoons grated fresh ginger

¼ teaspoon asafoetida powder (see page 71)

Juice of 2 limes

In traditional mango pickles, mangos are usually sun-dried to concentrate their flavors. I learned a quick trick from *Burma Superstar: Addictive Recipes from the Crossroads of Southeast Asia* by Desmond Tan and Kate Leahy: Dehydrate them in a low-heat oven for the same effect. In India, green mangos are bred specifically for pickling. Here in the United States, mangos like Kent or Tommy Atkins are completely green when unripe and turn yellow/red as they ripen. They are larger and not as sour. If you can't find green mangos, look for the most underripe ones possible and make up for it with more lime juice.

1. Wash all your equipment with hot, soapy water. Preheat the oven to 200°F.

2. MAKE THE PICKLE: On a large baking sheet, toss the mangos with the salt, chili powder, cumin, turmeric, and coriander. Bake undisturbed for 2 hours to dehydrate the mangos and infuse them with the spices. The mango skin will curl at the edges. Transfer to a large nonreactive bowl.

3. TEMPER THE PICKLE: For tempering, in a small dry skillet, toast the fenugreek and mustard seeds over medium heat until they start to pop and release their fragrance, 30 seconds to 1 minute. Grind with a spice grinder or with a mortar and pestle.

4. Using the same skillet over medium heat, warm the oil. Add the garlic and ginger, and cook until golden, about 1 minute. Remove from the heat. Stir in the fenugreek-mustard mixture and the asafoetida. Set aside to cool completely.

5. When the seasoned oil has cooled, pour it over the mangos and gently mix. Spoon the mango pickle into a quart-size glass jar (at least 2 cups), leaving a ½-inch headspace. Squeeze in the lime juice, cap the jar tightly, and shake well. Keep at room temperature for 2 days, or up to 1 week, shaking the jar daily to evenly distribute the spices, and then refrigerate. This mango pickle keeps for up to 6 months in the refrigerator.

SWITCH IT UP: Try this basic recipe with other vegetables like chopped cauliflower or carrots, but skip the dehydrating. Blanch the vegetables first, if you prefer. Add some brown sugar to the mix, too, if you like sweet-savory flavors.

SWEET, SOUR, AND SPICY MANGO SAUCE | AMBA

INDIA/ISRAEL

Makes: 2 cups | Prep and Cook time: 15 minutes | Fermenting time: 5 to 10 days | Curing time: 24 hours

4 cups firm, unripe mangos, peeled and cut into 1-inch cubes (1½ to 2 pounds or 2 mangos)

2 tablespoons coarse sea salt or kosher salt

4 cups warm water, divided, plus more as needed

1 teaspoon mustard seeds

1 teaspoon fenugreek seeds

1 tablespoon vegetable oil

2 garlic cloves, sliced

1 small fresh red or green chile, like Thai, chopped (optional)

1 teaspoon ground cumin

¼ teaspoon hot red chili powder, like cayenne

¼ teaspoon sweet smoked paprika

1 teaspoon ground turmeric

2 tablespoons brown sugar

Juice and zest of 1 large lime

While amba sauce is a popular condiment at falafel stands in Israel, its undeniable similarity to Indian mango pickle reveals its Indian heritage. Apparently, the sauce was invented by Iraqi Jews living in Bombay during the 19th century and was brought to Israel in the 1950s. Today, amba is often used as a dressing for shawarma sandwiches and always on the popular Israeli sabich sandwich.

1. Wash all your equipment with hot, soapy water.

2. Pack the mangos into 2 quart-size jars. Stir the salt into 2 cups warm water until it dissolves completely. Divide this brine between the jars. Place a weight on top of the mangos and seal. Ferment for 5 to 10 days at room temperature. Burp daily for the first few days to release the pressure from the carbon dioxide.

3. When the mangos are fermented to your liking (they should taste a little tart and pungent), drain in a colander and discard the brine.

4. In a dry medium saucepan over medium-high heat, toast the mustard seeds and fenugreek seeds until they start to pop and smell fragrant, 2 to 3 minutes. Watch carefully so they don't burn. Remove from the heat and grind in a spice grinder or with a mortar and pestle. Set aside.

5. Pour the vegetable oil into the same saucepan and warm over medium heat. Add the garlic and fresh chile (if using) and stir, cooking until the garlic is light golden but not browned, about 1 minute. Add the cumin, chili powder, paprika, and turmeric. Stir and cook for 1 more minute.

6. Add the mangos, sugar, and remaining 2 cups water and adjust the heat to a simmer. Cook for 5 to 6 minutes, until the mangos have softened and the mixture has reduced a little. Remove from the heat, and add the lime juice and zest and additional salt to taste. Taste and adjust the seasonings if desired. Set aside to cool for a few minutes.

7. Pour the mixture into a blender, or use an immersion blender. Puree until smooth. Add some water to thin the sauce if desired.

8. Pour the sauce into a pint-size jar and cure for 24 hours in the refrigerator. The sauce will keep in the refrigerator for 3 months.

   TRY IT WITH: Serve amba as a sauce for chicken or grilled tofu, as a replacement for hot sauce in tacos, or on a hamburger.

FIERY LIME PICKLE | NIMBU KA ACHAAR

INDIA

Makes: 2 pints | **Prep and Cook time:** 30 minutes, plus 2 hours sitting time |
Fermenting time: 2 weeks

FOR THE PICKLE

2 pounds limes, preferably
    thin-skinned and organic
    (about 15 large limes)
5 garlic cloves, minced
1 (2-inch) piece fresh ginger,
    peeled and grated
2 tablespoons coarse sea salt
    or kosher salt
2 tablespoons sugar (optional)
¼ cup mild red chili powder,
    like Kashmiri
2 teaspoons ground turmeric
2 teaspoons ground
    fenugreek seeds
1 teaspoon asafoetida powder
    (see the ingredient tip)

FOR TEMPERING

2 tablespoons vegetable oil
1 teaspoon mustard seeds
1 teaspoon fenugreek seeds
10 curry leaves
4 small dried red chiles, like
    chiles de arbol, broken
    into pieces

Lime pickle is one of India's most popular condiments. It is often eaten with rice, parathas, and/or lentils. There are many recipes for lime pickle; several require salting and fermenting the limes in the sun for several weeks until they turn brown, before tossing them with spices and tempering oil. I'm impatient and didn't do that. For variety, you can also use lemons or Key limes. If you don't like it too spicy, replace up to 2 tablespoons of the chili powder with paprika.

1. Wash all your equipment with hot, soapy water.

2. MAKE THE PICKLE: Scrub the limes to remove wax and dirt. Cut 10 limes into eighths and put them into a large nonreactive bowl. Halve the remaining 5 limes and squeeze their juice into the bowl.

3. Add the garlic, ginger, salt, sugar (if using), chili powder, turmeric, fenugreek, and asafoetida to the bowl.

4. Mix well with gloved hands and cover the bowl with plastic wrap. Set aside for 2 hours, or up to 12 hours.

5. TEMPER THE PICKLE: In a small skillet over medium heat, warm the oil. Add the mustard seeds and fenugreek seeds. When the seeds start to pop and release their fragrance, 30 seconds to 1 minute, add the curry leaves and red chiles and stir for about 1 minute. Remove from the heat and set aside to cool.

6. When the spices have cooled completely, add them to the bowl and mix well. Scoop the lime pickle into 2 pint-size jars, leaving ½ inch of headspace.

7. Keep the jars at room temperature in a location with plenty of sunlight. Invert the jars every day to distribute the contents evenly. Ferment for at least 2 weeks, or longer if possible. Lime pickle will keep in the refrigerator for at least 1 year.

INGREDIENT TIP: Asafoetida (also called "hing") is an Indian spice that flavors soups, vegetable dishes, pickles, and relishes. It is a dried resin that comes from three giant fennel species. Sold as a powder, asafoetida has a strong, pungent smell and tastes bitter and musky on its own. But once it's cooked in oil, it becomes pleasantly onionlike. You can find it at Indian markets.

SRI LANKAN CHILE PASTE | KATTA SAMBOL

SRI LANKA
Makes: 1½ cups | Prep time: 10 minutes

2 cups coarsely chopped
   shallot or red onion
   (6 ounces)
8 small dried red chiles,
   like chiles de arbol, or
   3 tablespoons red chili flakes
¼ teaspoon coarse sea salt or
   kosher salt
10 curry leaves
1 tablespoon Maldive fish
   chips (optional, see the
   ingredient tip)
2 teaspoons freshly squeezed
   lime juice
Red chili powder, like cayenne,
   for color

This Sri Lankan chile paste is much like the chile pastes of other Asian countries. It is eaten with traditional foods like coconut milk rice, hoppers, and roti (flatbread).

In a food processor, combine the shallots, chiles, and salt. Blitz until a coarse paste forms. Add the curry leaves and the fish chips (if using), and blitz again until you reach your desired consistency. Spoon into a bowl and add the lime juice. Mix well and taste. Add more salt or lime juice if desired. Sprinkle with the red chili powder for color.

INGREDIENT TIP: Maldive fish chips (umbalakada) are small chips of dried tuna that are a staple of Sri Lankan cuisine. They are a flavor enhancer and thickening agent and can be replaced with fish sauce or shrimp paste, or you can opt to eliminate them for a vegetarian sambai. They are available online or at any store that carries Sri Lankan foods.

PLUM SAUCE (OR DUCK SAUCE)

CHINA

Makes: 2 pints | **Prep time:** 20 minutes | **Cook time:** 30 to 45 minutes

2 pounds plums and/or apricots, pitted and coarsely chopped

½ cup chopped yellow onion (4 ounces)

2 garlic cloves, chopped

2 tablespoons grated fresh ginger

1 fresh long red chile, like Fresno or serrano, chopped

½ cup apple cider vinegar or distilled white vinegar

1 cup sugar

1 teaspoon coarse sea salt or kosher salt

1 teaspoon Chinese five-spice powder

Plum sauce is also called duck sauce, because it often accompanies roasted duck. A staple at Chinese restaurants in the United States, plum sauce is used as a dipping sauce for fried egg rolls and wonton strips. It also makes a good stir-fry sauce.

1. In a medium pot over medium-high heat, combine the plums, onion, garlic, ginger, chile, vinegar, sugar, salt, and five-spice powder and bring to a boil. Adjust the heat and simmer for 30 to 45 minutes, until the plums have broken down and the sauce thickens. Stir often to keep the bottom from burning. Taste and adjust the seasonings if desired.

2. Use an immersion blender to puree into a smooth sauce, or pour the mixture into a food processor or blender and puree it until smooth. You may need to do this in batches. Set it aside to cool. Ladle the sauce into pint-size jars. The sauce can be eaten immediately or kept in the refrigerator for up to 4 weeks.

YES YOU CAN! Plum sauce can be canned so that it keeps for up to 1 year on the shelf. Following the canning instructions on page 15, ladle hot plum sauce into pint-size jars that have been washed with hot, soapy water, leaving a ¼-inch headspace. Remove any air bubbles, wipe the rims, and seal the jars. Process in a water-bath canner for 15 minutes. Wait 5 minutes before removing the jars, and check the seals after 12 to 24 hours.

BANANA KETCHUP

PHILIPPINES
Makes: 1½ cups | **Prep time:** 10 minutes | **Cook time:** 30 minutes

2 tablespoons vegetable oil

2 garlic cloves, chopped

½ cup chopped onion

1 teaspoon grated fresh ginger

2 tablespoons tomato paste

¼ cup rice vinegar

½ cup water

1 cup bananas, mashed
  (2 bananas)

2 Thai red chiles, seeded and
  chopped (optional)

2 tablespoons light
  brown sugar

1 teaspoon coarse sea salt or
  kosher salt

½ teaspoon freshly ground
  black pepper

1 clove, crushed

¼ teaspoon ground paprika

⅛ teaspoon ground cinnamon

Banana ketchup is a condiment unique to the Philippines. It was invented during World War II, when tomatoes were scarce and bananas plentiful in the Philippines. To make it resemble traditional ketchup, red dye is sometimes added. It is used very much like tomato ketchup on hot dogs, hamburgers, and fried chicken, and sometimes in Filipino spaghetti sauce. Don't be afraid of the long ingredients list—you likely have most of these items on hand already.

1. In a medium saucepan over medium heat, warm the oil. Add the garlic, onion, and ginger. Stir and cook for 4 to 5 minutes, until soft and fragrant.

2. Reduce the heat to medium-low and add the tomato paste. Stir and cook until the paste turns a shade or two darker and smells fragrant. Add the vinegar and water and deglaze the pan, stirring to scrape up the brown bits from the bottom.

3. Add the bananas, chiles (if using), brown sugar, salt, black pepper, clove, paprika, and cinnamon. Mix well, raise the heat to medium-high, and bring the mixture to a gentle boil. Adjust the heat and simmer for 20 to 30 minutes, until the mixture thickens slightly.

4. Remove from the heat and set aside to cool for 5 to 10 minutes. Use an immersion blender or transfer the mixture to the bowl of a food processor or blender. Blitz until smooth. Add water to thin the ketchup if necessary. Taste and adjust the seasonings if desired.

5. Pour the banana ketchup into a pint-size jar. It will keep for 3 months in the refrigerator.

YES YOU CAN! While it's not traditional, banana ketchup can be canned so it keeps for up to 1 year on the shelf. Double the recipe. Following the canning instructions on page 15, ladle hot ketchup into 6 half-pint jars that have been washed in hot, soapy water, leaving a ½-inch headspace. Remove any air bubbles, wipe the rims, and seal the jars. Process in a water-bath canner for 15 minutes. Wait 5 minutes before removing the jars, and check the seals after 12 to 24 hours.

FERMENTED WHITE TOFU | BAI FU RU

CHINA

Makes: 8 ounces | **Prep time:** 15 minutes, plus 2 hours pressing time | **Fermenting time:** 2 to 5 days | **Curing time:** 4 weeks

½ (14- to 16-ounce) block firm or extra-firm tofu

1½ tablespoons fine sea salt

½ teaspoon red chili flakes, crushed Sichuan peppercorns, or crushed fennel seeds (optional)

½ cup water

¼ cup Chinese rice wine

Traditionally, fermented tofu is used as a condiment in cooking, with rice, or to flavor stir-fries; it adds tons of umami to any dish. I never thought of fermenting tofu at home until I saw a recipe in *Asian Tofu: Discover the Best, Make Your Own, and Cook It at Home*, a delightful cookbook by Andrea Nguyen. Now I can make my own fermented tofu using organic tofu without the nasty preservatives. This recipe is based on Andrea's.

1. Wash all your equipment with hot, soapy water.

2. Press the tofu to remove excess water. Wrap it in a thick non-terry-cloth kitchen towel or several layers of cheesecloth and place it between two cutting boards. Weigh it down with a heavy book, a cast-iron skillet, or canned goods. After about 2 hours, unwrap the tofu. It should feel slightly moist to the touch and very firm. Blot the block with paper towels and cut it into 1-inch cubes.

3. In a large rectangular glass container, place the tofu cubes spaced ½ inch to 1 inch apart. You want to be able to observe for mold growth. Cover tightly with plastic wrap and make 6 to 8 holes with a bamboo skewer for ventilation.

4. Keep the tofu at room temperature for 2 to 5 days, observing and smelling every day. Expect to see some condensation. The tofu is ready for the next step when it looks slick and wet, it is covered in orange-yellow mold, it smells pungent, and it is soft and a little creamy. The timing and the preceding indications depend on the temperature and climate. Furry, gray mold is okay. Just remove it before moving on.

5. When the tofu is ready, on a rimmed plate, mix together the salt and the chili flakes (if using). Using a gentle touch with a pair of chopsticks, lightly coat each tofu cube on all sides. In a 2-cup wide-mouth glass jar or bowl with a lid, lay the tofu cubes flat. It's okay if they are stacked.

6. In a measuring cup, combine the water and wine, and pour the mixture into the jar. If the tofu cubes are not fully submerged, mix more wine and water in the same ratio. Seal and refrigerate for at least 4 weeks before using. The longer you let it age, the stronger and softer it becomes. Try it weekly to see what stage you like it best. This will keep indefinitely in the refrigerator.

TRY IT WITH: Mash fermented tofu together with lime juice, sugar, and chile paste for a delectable dipping sauce. Or use it to flavor stir-fried water spinach and chiles.

LEMONGRASS CHILE SAUCE

SINGAPORE

Makes: 1 cup | **Prep time:** 20 minutes | **Cook time:** 40 minutes

2 cups fresh long red chiles, like Fresno or red serrano, seeded and chopped (½ pound)

2 lemongrass stalks, bulbs only, roughly chopped (see the ingredient tip)

3 garlic cloves

1 (1-inch) piece fresh ginger, peeled and chopped

Pinch coarse sea salt or kosher salt, plus ¼ teaspoon

½ cup water

¼ cup fresh lime juice (from 1 large lime)

2 tablespoons sugar

2 tablespoons fish sauce

Hainanese chicken rice is a signature hawker dish in Singapore. Singapore is famous for its hawker centers, where individual stall owners (hawkers) sell food that they call hawker dishes. In that famous dish, delicately poached chicken is served with flavorful rice cooked in chicken stock and a delicious chile-garlic sauce that I could eat straight. I have always loved the lemony flavor and fragrance of lemongrass, and one day I decided to add some zest to the basic chile-garlic sauce recipe. Now I happily drizzle this sauce over everything.

1. In a food processor, combine the chiles, lemongrass, garlic, and ginger with a pinch of salt and blitz to confetti-size bits.

2. In a small nonreactive saucepan, combine the chile mixture with the water, lime juice, sugar, and remaining ¼ teaspoon of salt. Bring the mixture just to a boil over medium-high heat, then adjust the heat and simmer for 30 minutes, until the lemongrass and chiles soften.

3. Remove from the heat and add the fish sauce. Serve immediately. This sauce keeps in the refrigerator for 1 week.

INGREDIENT TIP: Fresh lemongrass is available in the produce section of Asian markets and sometimes at grocery stores in the specialty foods section. Choose lemongrass stalks that are fat, firm, fragrant, and look fresh, with no mold or mildew. To use, discard the dry outer leaves, then cut off about 1 inch from the root end and the fibrous top, leaving the tender middle section, which is essentially the bulb. Use only the bulb in this recipe, and save the rest to flavor tea or soups (or use in Pickled Shallots, page 129).

MOMO SAUCE

NEPAL

Makes: 1 cup | **Prep time:** 10 minutes | **Cook time:** 20 minutes

Vegetable oil, for coating
   and drizzling
½ pound Roma tomatoes,
   halved (4 or 5 tomatoes)
2 garlic cloves
1 (½-inch) piece ginger,
   peeled and coarsely chopped
3 or 4 small dried red chiles,
   like chiles de arbol, crushed
⅛ ounce whole blanched or
   roasted almonds (5 almonds)
1 tablespoon sugar
1 tablespoon soy sauce
1 tablespoon freshly squeezed
   lemon juice
½ cup loosely packed
   cilantro leaves
Water, as needed
Salt (optional)

Momos are round meat or vegetable dumplings, similar to Chinese baozi. They are popular in Nepal, Tibet, and India. Unlike Chinese dumplings, which are usually accompanied by a soy-vinegar-based dipping sauce, momos are served with this piquant tomato-based sauce. The almonds are used as a thickener. For a nut-free version, substitute 1 tablespoon sesame seeds.

1. Preheat the oven to 450°F.

2. Coat a nonreactive baking dish with oil. Place the tomatoes cut-side down and drizzle with more oil. Roast for 10 minutes. Toss the garlic into the dish with the tomatoes and roast for 8 to 10 more minutes, until the garlic and tomatoes are browned but not black. Remove from the oven and set aside to cool.

3. When the tomatoes and garlic are cool, place them in the bowl of a food processor or blender. Add the ginger, chiles, almonds, sugar, soy sauce, and lemon juice. Pulse until the ginger and almonds have broken up into small pieces. Add the cilantro, then blend until a smooth sauce forms. Add water as needed to loosen the sauce.

4. Pour the sauce into a small bowl. Taste and add salt if desired. Serve immediately or refrigerate for up to 2 days.

TRY IT WITH: This sauce is also delicious as a salad dressing and as a dip for tortilla chips.

KOREAN RED PEPPER PASTE | GOCHUJANG

KOREA

Makes: 10 to 12 cups | **Prep time:** 5 minutes, plus 2 hours sitting time | **Cook time:** 1 hour 15 minutes | **Fermenting time:** 2 to 3 months

8 cups water

2 cups barley malt powder

5 cups sweet rice flour
   (glutinous rice flour)

3 cups brown rice syrup

1 cup fermented soy flour

6 cups finely ground Korean
   red pepper powder

¾ cup coarse sea salt or
   kosher salt

Korean red pepper paste, or gochujang, is used extensively in Korean cooking. You can find it in huge tubs at the Asian market. But as you'll learn from this recipe, once you have the ingredients, it's not hard to make, and the flavor of the fresh stuff is miles better. The hardest parts are finding the ingredients and waiting! You can find all of the ingredients at a Korea-centric Asian market like H-Mart. Please read the labels carefully to make sure you're buying the right ingredients: barley malt powder (yeotgireum), sweet rice flour (also called mochiko or glutinous rice flour; Koda Farms is a California-based brand), fermented soy flour (mejugaru), and finely ground Korean red pepper powder (gochujaru).

1. Wash all your equipment with hot, soapy water.

2. Heat the water in a large pot until it reaches a temperature of about 100°F (just above body temperature). Whisk in the barley malt powder until smooth, then whisk in the sweet rice flour, 1 cup at a time, whisking until all the lumps disappear before adding the next cup. Set aside for 2 hours.

3. Return the pot to the stove and cook at medium-low heat until reduced by one-third, 1 to 2 hours. Stir often to prevent the mixture from sticking to the bottom of the pot. Set aside to cool completely.

4. Once the mixture is cool, stir in the rice syrup, fermented soy flour, red pepper powder, and salt. Mix thoroughly, using the back of a wooden spoon to smooth out any lumps, until the mixture is shiny and creamy.

5. Scoop the red pepper paste into a gallon-size jar or fermenting crock. Cover with cheesecloth and secure with a rubber band. Place the lid on the jar or crock. Set by a sunny window and ferment at room temperature. When it's sunny, remove the lid to expose the paste to some heat and sunshine through the cheesecloth. This will help prevent mold from forming. If mold does form on the surface, scrape it off, then add a teaspoon or two of salt and mix everything up. To prevent more mold from forming, you can also sprinkle a layer of salt over the top of the paste.

6. Move the jar to a cooler location in the afternoons, out of direct sunlight. Ferment for 2 to 3 months. Once the gochujang is fermented to your liking, transfer to one or more containers with tight-fitting lids and store in the refrigerator for up to 1 year.

INGREDIENT TIP: Ground Korean red pepper comes in two different grades: fine powder and coarse flakes. In terms of flavor, they are similar. Fine powder is used to make gochujang and other sauces for a brighter color and a smooth texture. Coarse flakes are most often used to make kimchi. Korean red pepper comes in bags of at least 1 pound. Store them in a cool, dry place, away from sunlight.

CHAPTER 4

Kimchi and Other Fermented Vegetables

Classic Cabbage Kimchi | Baechu Kimchi 86

Green Onion Kimchi | Pa Kimchi 89

Easy Kimchi | Mak Kimchi 90

White Kimchi | Baek Kimchi 92

Broccoli Rabe Kimchi 94

Rice Bran Pickles | Nukazuke 96

Quick Cucumber Kimchi 99

Bitter Greens Kimchi 100

Fermented Yellow Radish | Takuan 102

Salted Rice Koji Pickles | Shio Koji Asazuke 104

Shan Pickles | Mon-Nyin Chin 106

Salt-Pickled Mustard Cabbage | Suan Cai 108

Sichuan Pickles | Pao Cai 110

Daikon and Jicama Water Kimchi | Dongchimi 111

Red Vegetable Kimchi 112

Miso-Ginger Sauerkraut 114

Fermented Eggplant | Ca Phao Muoi 116

PICKLE PASSPORT: KOREA

Must-try pickles: Classic Cabbage Kimchi (page 86),
Easy Kimchi (page 90), Daikon and Jicama Water Kimchi (page 111),
Sesame Zucchini Threads (page 41), Korean Red Pepper Paste (page 80)

The earliest record of kimchi is in the *Book of Odes*, China's oldest poetry collection, written nearly 3,000 years ago, but it is Koreans who have always valued strong, complex flavors above the other cardinal tastes of sweet, sour, bitter, and salty. Korean food has a unique pungency, which is the sharp, tangy flavor found in pickles (kimchi) and other condiments, such as soybean paste and chile paste. This flavor, the result of controlled fermentation, is distinctive of Korean cuisine.

Korean cuisine is synonymous with kimchi (sometimes spelled kimchee). The fiery fermented condiment we know today only became widespread during the 18th century, nearly 200 years after chile peppers were introduced to Korea. Before chile peppers were introduced, the strong flavors of mustard and black pepper were popular. Korean pickles were often pickled in a brine steeped with Japanese pepper or fennel seeds, but Koreans realized that chile peppers helped preserve vegetables and eliminated the use of excessive amounts of salt.

Kimchi plays a very important role in Korean culture. Every fall, Koreans gather with friends, family, and neighbors for gimjang (or kimjang) to prepare large quantities of kimchi to last through the winter. Modern kimchi is typically made with Chinese (napa) cabbage, daikon radishes, and green onions, but there are hundreds of variations. Just about any vegetable can be kimchi-fied, and the results aren't always spicy.

A traditional Korean meal wouldn't be complete without banchan (or panchan). Banchan is the collective name for the assorted small side dishes served with rice, soup, and meats. They are meant to be shared and finished during the meal. Many different dishes can be served as banchan, including kimchi, seasoned vegetables, stir-fried vegetables, and savory pancakes.

CLASSIC CABBAGE KIMCHI | BAECHU KIMCHI

KOREA

Makes: 1 quart | Prep time: 45 minutes, plus 2 to 3 hours salting time | Cook time: 10 minutes | Fermenting time: 8 hours to 2 days

FOR THE CABBAGE

3 pounds Chinese (napa) cabbage (1 medium cabbage)

¼ cup coarse sea salt or kosher salt (1¼ ounces)

FOR THE KIMCHI PASTE

1 cup water

1 tablespoon sweet rice (glutinous rice) flour or rice flour

1 tablespoon sugar (optional)

3 tablespoons minced garlic (12 cloves)

2 teaspoons minced fresh ginger (¼ ounce)

½ cup chopped onion (1 small onion)

2 tablespoons fish sauce

2 tablespoons fermented salted shrimp (saeujeot) with the salty brine, chopped (substitute more fish sauce, if preferred)

¼ to ½ cup Korean red pepper flakes (gochujaru), depending on taste

1 cup daikon radish, cut into matchsticks (4 ounces)

½ cup carrot, cut into matchsticks (1 ounce)

1½ cups green onion, chopped into 1-inch pieces (6 stalks)

In late fall, Korean households make this traditional cabbage kimchi recipe in large quantities for gimjang (or kimjang), an annual kimchi-making event in preparation for the cold months. Relatives, neighbors, and friends gather for this laborious process. In traditional Korean households, cabbage kimchi is usually made in large batches (10 to 15 heads at a time), but my recipe is for just one head—that's all I can handle eating at a time. If you'd like to make more, just double or triple the recipe.

The sweet rice "porridge" helps bind the kimchi paste together for easy spreading and is also believed to diminish the raw, bitter flavor of dark green vegetables like mustard greens or dandelion greens (see Bitter Greens Kimchi, page 100). The porridge also serves as food for beneficial lactic acid bacteria and hastens the fermenting process. You don't have to use it. Omit it to keep the kimchi "fresh" tasting.

1. Wash all your equipment in hot, soapy water.

2. PREP THE CABBAGE: Make a shallow cut (about one-third of the way through) lengthwise from the base of the cabbage to the leafy top end. Don't cut all the way through. Cutting the cabbage all the way through would damage the tender inner leaves. Gently pull the cabbage apart into halves, keeping the inner leaves intact. You want the leaves loose but still attached to the core. Then make similar cuts in each cabbage half, but don't pull them apart yet.

3. Put the cabbage in a large nonreactive bowl. Lift every leaf up, one by one, and sprinkle the salt in between the leaves, using more salt at the base of the stem near the core. Continue until the entire cabbage is covered and all the salt is used up.

4. Set the cabbage aside for 2 to 3 hours. Flip every 30 minutes or so, shuffling the cabbage at the bottom of the bowl to the top and vice versa. The cabbage is ready when the leaves are soft and bendable.

5. Rinse the cabbage under cold running water to remove excess salt. Gently split the halves with your hands into quarters along the slits you cut earlier. Drain the cabbage in a colander.

6. MAKE THE PASTE: In a medium saucepan over medium heat, bring the water to a gentle boil. Add the sweet rice flour and cook for 8 to 10 minutes, stirring with a wooden spoon or spatula, until it starts to thicken into a thin porridge. Remove from the heat and stir in the sugar (if using) until it dissolves completely. Set aside to cool.

7. Wearing a pair of food-safe gloves, in a large nonreactive bowl, mix together the cooled porridge, garlic, ginger, onion, fish sauce, fermented salted shrimp (if using), and red pepper flakes to make the kimchi paste. Mix well until the mixture turns into a thin paste. Mix in the radish, carrot, and green onion. Taste and adjust the seasonings if desired. The paste should taste spicy, a little too salty to eat on its own, and a little sweet if you like.

8. Take one cabbage quarter and spread kimchi paste (1 to 2 tablespoons per cabbage leaf) in between the leaves. When every leaf is covered with paste, start at the leaf end and roll into a small packet. Place the packet into your fermenting vessel. Repeat until all the cabbage is done. Rinse your kimchi bowl with a little water (about 2 tablespoons) and pour

continued

this liquid into the jar. Press down firmly with your hands to remove any air bubbles. If the cabbage is not completely submerged, add a light brine made with 1 cup water and 1 tablespoon salt. Place a weight (see page 14 for examples) on top of the vegetables to keep them submerged under the brine. Wrap the mouth of the vessel with plastic wrap and ferment at room temperature away from direct sunlight for at least 8 hours. The kimchi will release liquid as it ferments, so place the vessel on a plate to catch any spills.

9. Once the kimchi is fermented to your liking, cover the vessel and store in the refrigerator. (I keep the plastic wrap on to prevent smells from leaking out.) It will continue to ferment slowly and will keep in the refrigerator for months.

PREP TIP: Chop the garlic, ginger, and onion in a food processor. Then mix in the fish sauce, fermented shrimp, red pepper, and porridge.

DON'T FORGET: Always wear food-safe gloves when handling the red pepper flakes. The gloves will prevent chili burn and also keep you from hurting yourself if you rub your eyes.

FERMENTING TIP: When you've finished packing the kimchi into the fermenting vessel, ferment at room temperature for at least 8 hours in summer, 12 hours in winter. For me, kimchi tastes best when fermented for at least 24 hours if warm, 48 hours if cold. The best thing to do is taste every day to determine when the kimchi tastes most pleasing to you. Store in the refrigerator, and the kimchi will continue to ferment and turn sour.

GREEN ONION KIMCHI | PA KIMCHI

KOREA

Makes: 1 pint | **Prep time:** 15 minutes | **Fermenting time:** 2 hours to 3 days

1 pound green onions

1 tablespoon minced garlic

2 teaspoons minced fresh ginger

¼ cup fish sauce

2 teaspoons sugar

2 to 4 tablespoons Korean red pepper flakes (gochujaru), depending on taste

Calling all allium fans, this kimchi is for you. In this recipe, green onions, also called scallions or spring onions, are the stars. If the onion-y flavor is too much for you, tone it down by adding a cup of shredded carrots for sweetness, or heat it up by tossing in some chopped fresh red chiles.

1. Wash all your equipment in hot, soapy water.

2. Cut off the roots of the green onions and any tough or brown outer leaves.

3. Wearing a pair of food-safe gloves, in a large nonreactive bowl, mix together the garlic, ginger, fish sauce, sugar, and red pepper flakes to make the kimchi paste. Add a little water if the paste is too dry. Taste and adjust the seasonings if desired. The paste should taste spicy, a little too salty to eat on its own, and a little sweet if you like.

4. Toss the green onions with the kimchi paste until well coated. Grab a couple of stalks and fold them into a bundle. Pack the bundle into a pint-size jar and repeat until all the green onions have been folded and packed into the jar.

5. Ferment at room temperature away from direct sunlight for 2 hours, or up to 3 days. Once the kimchi is fermented to your liking, store it in the refrigerator. It will keep for 1 month.

6. To serve, run a knife or kitchen scissors through the folded bundles a few times.

SWITCH IT UP: Any allium with green leafy tops would work in this kimchi: ramps, chives, or garlic chives. Try mixing and matching.

EASY KIMCHI | MAK KIMCHI

KOREA

Makes: 1½ pints | **Prep time:** 20 minutes, plus 2 to 3 hours salting time | **Fermenting time:** 8 hours

3 pounds Chinese (napa)
  cabbage (1 medium cabbage)
¼ cup coarse sea salt
2 tablespoons minced garlic
1 tablespoon minced
  fresh ginger
2 tablespoons fish sauce
1 teaspoon sugar, or to taste
¼ to ½ cup Korean red
  pepper flakes (gochujaru),
  depending on taste
1 cup green onion, cut into
  1-inch pieces (4 stalks)

The Korean word *mak* means "carelessly" or "roughly." I wouldn't say this is a careless recipe per se, but I would say that it is an easier recipe than the traditional one and is my preferred way of making kimchi. Cutting the cabbage first makes it easier to handle, and this recipe does away with the use of the porridge. Most important, this version is just as tasty.

1. Wash all your equipment with hot, soapy water.

2. Halve the cabbage and cut a "V" notch at the base to remove the core. Cut into bite-size pieces. Put the cabbage in a large nonreactive bowl and sprinkle with the salt. Massage the salt into the cabbage and set aside for 2 to 3 hours, tossing every 30 minutes or so. The cabbage is ready when it has shrunk and is soft and bendable.

3. Rinse the cabbage under cold running water to remove any excess salt, and drain in a colander.

4. Wearing a pair of food-safe gloves, in a large nonreactive bowl, mix together the garlic, ginger, fish sauce, sugar, and red pepper flakes to make the kimchi paste. Add a little water if the paste is too dry. Add the green onions.

5. Toss the cabbage with the kimchi paste until well coated. Taste and adjust the seasonings if desired. The paste should taste spicy, a little too salty to eat on its own, and a little sweet if you like.

6. Pack the cabbage into a quart-size jar, leaving 2 inches of headspace. Rinse the bowl with a little water (about 2 tablespoons) and pour this liquid into the jar. Push down firmly with your hands to remove any air bubbles. Place a weight (see page 14 for examples) on top of the vegetables to keep them submerged under the brine. Wrap the mouth of the jar with plastic wrap and ferment at room temperature away from direct sunlight for at least 8 hours. The kimchi will release liquid as it ferments, so place the jar on a plate to catch any spills.

7. Once the kimchi is fermented to your liking, cap the jar and store in the refrigerator. (I keep the plastic wrap on to prevent smells from leaking out.) It will continue to ferment slowly and will keep in the refrigerator for months.

SWITCH IT UP: Make this kimchi vegetarian. Just take out the fish sauce and use soy sauce or miso paste in its place. If you have both, you can use a mix of red pepper powder and coarser flakes to make kimchi.

WHITE KIMCHI | BAEK KIMCHI

KOREA

Makes: 1 quart | **Prep time:** 30 minutes, plus 2 to 3 hours salting time |
Fermenting time: 12 to 24 hours | **Curing time:** 3 days

FOR THE CABBAGE

3 pounds Chinese (napa)
    cabbage (1 medium cabbage)
¼ cup coarse sea salt or
    kosher salt (1¼ ounces)

FOR THE BRINE

4 cups water
2 teaspoons coarse sea salt or
    kosher salt
1 teaspoon sugar (optional)
1 tablespoon minced garlic
1 teaspoon minced
    fresh ginger

FOR THE KIMCHI FILLING

1 tablespoon sugar
1 teaspoon fish sauce
2 cups daikon radish, peeled
    and cut into matchsticks
    (4 ounces)
1 cup carrot, cut into
    matchsticks (2 ounces)
1 cup pear or apple, cut into
    matchsticks (2 ounces)
1 cup green onion, cut into
    1-inch pieces, white and pale
    green parts only (6 stalks)
¼ cup sliced red bell pepper
    (1 ounce)
4 pitted dried red dates, thinly
    sliced, or 2 tablespoons goji
    berries (optional)
1 tablespoon pine nuts
    (optional)

Not all kimchi has to be spicy. White kimchi is a variation on kimchi that's made without red pepper flakes. But that doesn't mean it's not still full of flavor. It has a mild, refreshing taste that's child friendly and appealing to adults who are spice-averse. This kimchi doesn't keep as long as other varieties, so eat it within a few weeks.

1. Wash all your equipment with hot, soapy water.

2. PREP THE CABBAGE: Make a shallow cut (about one-third of the way through) lengthwise from the base of the cabbage to the leafy top end. Don't cut all the way through. Cutting the cabbage all the way through would damage the tender inner leaves. Gently pull the cabbage apart into halves, keeping the inner leaves intact. You want the leaves loose but still attached to the core. Then make similar cuts for each half, but don't pull them apart yet.

3. Place the cabbage in a large nonreactive bowl. Lift every leaf up, one by one, and sprinkle the salt in between the leaves, using more salt at the base of the stem near the core. Continue until the entire cabbage is covered and all the salt is used up. Place a heavy plate on top of the cabbage to weigh it down.

4. Set the cabbage aside for 2 to 3 hours. Flip every 30 minutes or so, shuffling the cabbage at the bottom of the bowl to the top and vice versa. The cabbage is ready when the leaves are soft and bendable.

5. Rinse the cabbage under cold running water to remove any excess salt. Gently split the halves into quarters with your fingers along the slits you cut earlier. Drain the cabbage in a colander.

6. MAKE THE BRINE: In a large nonreactive bowl, stir together the water, salt, sugar (if using), garlic, and ginger, until the salt and sugar dissolve completely.

7. MAKE THE FILLING: In another bowl, mix together the sugar, fish sauce, daikon, carrot, pear, green onion, bell pepper, red dates (if using), and pine nuts (if using).

8. Take one cabbage quarter and spread the filling (1 to 2 tablespoons per cabbage leaf) in between the leaves. When every leaf is covered with filling, place the filled cabbage quarter into the bowl with the brine. Repeat with the remaining cabbage and kimchi filling, and arrange the filled cabbage quarters in the bowl as snugly as possible.

9. Place a heavy plate on top of the cabbage to keep it submerged under the brine, and ferment at room temperature away from direct sunlight for 12 hours in summer or 24 hours in winter. Remove the plate, cover, and store in the refrigerator with the brine for up to 3 weeks.

10. White kimchi tastes best after at least 3 days in the refrigerator. To serve, remove a cabbage quarter, allowing excess brine to drip back into the container. Cut crosswise into 2-inch pieces and serve with a few scoops of brine.

BROCCOLI RABE KIMCHI

KOREA

Makes: 1 pint | **Prep time:** 15 minutes, plus 30 minutes salting time | **Fermenting time:** 24 hours

10 ounces broccoli rabe, cut into 1-inch pieces (1 bunch)

1 tablespoon coarse sea salt or kosher salt

1 tablespoon sugar (optional)

1 tablespoon minced garlic

2 teaspoons minced fresh ginger

1 tablespoon fish sauce

¼ to ½ cup Korean red pepper flakes (gochujaru), depending on taste

4 green onions, cut into 1-inch pieces

½ cup chopped red bell pepper (1 small pepper)

Salting vegetables has a twofold purpose: First, it acts as a preservative and draws water out, tenderizing the ingredients in the process. Additionally, the vegetables become porous, allowing the spices to infuse into them thoroughly—so don't skip this process!

1. Wash all your equipment with hot, soapy water.

2. In a large nonreactive bowl, toss the rabe with the salt and sugar (if using). Set aside for 30 minutes.

3. Meanwhile, in another large nonreactive bowl and wearing a pair of food-safe gloves, mix together the garlic, ginger, fish sauce, and Korean red pepper flakes to make the kimchi paste. Add a little water if the paste is too dry. Add the green onions and bell pepper. Taste and adjust the seasonings if desired. The paste should taste spicy, a little too salty to eat on its own, and a little sweet if you like.

4. Rinse the rabe under cold running water and drain in a colander. Toss the rabe with the kimchi paste until well coated. The kimchi is ready to eat immediately but will taste even better after fermentation.

5. To ferment, pack the rabe into a pint-size jar, leaving 2 inches of headspace. Rinse the bowl with a little water (2 tablespoons) and pour this liquid into the jar. Push down firmly with your hands to remove any air bubbles. Place a weight (see page 14 for options) on top of the vegetables to keep them submerged under the brine. Wrap the mouth of the jar with plastic wrap

and ferment at room temperature away from direct sunlight for 24 hours. The kimchi will release liquid as it ferments, so place the jar on a plate to catch any spills.

6. Once the kimchi is fermented to your liking, cap the jar and store in the refrigerator. (I keep the plastic wrap on to prevent smells from leaking out.) It will continue to ferment slowly and will keep in the refrigerator for up to 1 month.

RICE BRAN PICKLES | NUKAZUKE

JAPAN

Makes: 4 cups rice bran mixture for the pickling bed (enough for pickling almost indefinitely) |
Prep time: 55 minutes | **Cook time:** 5 minutes | **Bed Curing time:** 2½ weeks |
Vegetable Pickling time: 6 to 12 hours

FOR THE PICKLING BED

4 cups rice bran

¼ cup coarse sea salt or
  kosher salt

1⅔ cups water

1 (1-inch) square piece of
  kombu, cut into strips

2 dried shiitake mushroom
  stems or 1 small broken cap

1 garlic clove

1 (½-inch) piece fresh ginger,
  cut into 2 or 3 slices

1 or 2 dried red chiles, like
  chiles de arbol, halved

½ cup veggie scraps, like
  daikon peels, ginger peels,
  turnip tops, or small chunks
  of vegetables (just no onions
  or potatoes)

FOR THE PICKLES

2 small carrots, peeled and
  halved lengthwise

OR

2 small cucumbers (or other
  watery vegetables like celery),
  peeled, halved, rubbed with
  salt, rinsed, and dried

OR

6 baby turnips (like hakurei),
  peeled and halved

OR

8 small red radishes, whole

Rice bran pickling is a quintessential Japanese pickling method. Many Japanese households have a rice bran pickling bed (nukadoko) that they have been tending for a long time.

The first step in making rice bran pickles is to establish a live and active nukadoko. The three essential ingredients are bran, salt, and water. Additionally, you can add a variety of ingredients to amp up the flavor: garlic, ginger, kombu (dried seaweed), dried mushrooms. Adding fruit like dried apples or persimmon peels will add sweetness.

Next, the pickling bed has to be primed with starter vegetables. These can range from kitchen scraps to small chunks of vegetables like daikon or cucumber. The bacteria that live on the vegetable skins will help promote the growth of live (plant-generated) lactobacilli. Once your pickling bed has reached maturity, you can make probiotic-rich pickles in hours. Remember, the pickling bed must be stirred and mixed daily.

Depending on how long they are pickled and on the aromatics added to the pickling bed, rice bran pickles will taste anywhere from pleasantly tangy to sour and/or salty.

My recipe uses a smaller amount of rice bran suited for a small bed (I use a 6-by-10-by-4-inch ceramic container). Feel free to double the recipe for a larger nukadoko.

1. **MAKE THE PICKLING BED:** In a large skillet, spread the rice bran in a thin, even layer and dry roast over low heat. You'll have to do this in batches and repeat the process several times depending on the size of your pan. (I used a 10-inch cast-iron skillet and roasted 1 cup at a time.)

2. Stir the rice bran occasionally with a wooden spoon and jiggle the pan to keep the bran moving. After 1 to 2 minutes, the bran should start to darken. Dry roast for 2 to 3 minutes more, until the bran is heated through and smells slightly nutty. Watch carefully so it doesn't burn. Pour into a large mixing bowl. Repeat until all the bran has been roasted. When the bran is completely cool, it should feel dry and powdery. (If you can find roasted rice bran, you can skip this step.)

3. Wash all your equipment in hot, soapy water.

4. In a medium saucepan over medium-high heat, combine the salt and water and stir until the salt dissolves completely. Remove from the heat and set aside to cool to room temperature.

5. Add the brine to the roasted bran gradually, mixing with clean hands in between pours. Stop adding water when it forms a paste that feels like damp sand suitable for making sandcastles.

6. Pack half the bran mixture into your choice of pickle pot or container (see the prep tip for options). Scatter the kombu, mushroom, garlic, ginger, and chiles over and bury with the remaining bran mixture.

7. Cover the pickling bed loosely with several layers of cheesecloth or a kitchen towel, to allow airflow but keep out insects and debris. Keep the pickling bed at room temperature away from direct sunlight.

8. For the next 3 days, dig to the bottom of the container and flip and stir the paste with clean hands. Do this at least once a day, preferably two or three times, especially during the warmer months.

9. Now it's time to prime your pickling bed. Bury the vegetable scraps by pushing them deeply into the paste. Cover them completely by scraping the surrounding paste over them. If the scraps are small, tie them up in cheesecloth so they don't get lost.

continued

10. The next day, remove the scraps, scrape off as much bran as you can back into the container, and discard the scraps.

11. Repeat this process of burying and discarding the vegetable scraps daily, for at least 2 weeks. Flip and stir the paste before burying a new batch of scraps. Pack down the pickling bed so that it has a smooth surface, and wipe down the sides.

12. MAKE THE PICKLES: After 2 weeks, the pickling bed will have a pleasant, earthy smell and should be ready for pickling. Bury the vegetable pieces in the paste and leave them overnight. If they are still very salty the next day, pickle them for 1 to 2 more days.

13. Scrape as much bran as you can back into the pot and rinse the vegetables before eating.

14. When the pickle bed reaches maturity, vegetables are ready in 8 to 12 hours in the cooler months and 6 hours or less when it's hot outside (80°F and above).

15. Stir the pickling bed daily, whether or not you're pickling vegetables. If you can't do this daily, stir the pickling bed thoroughly, cover tightly, and store in the refrigerator until ready to resume.

PREP TIP: Nonreactive glass, enamel-lined metal, or glazed ceramic containers make the best pickle pots. If possible, choose a rectangular container, 5 to 6 inches long and 2 to 3 inches deep. This makes it easier to stir the bran without spilling. A tight-fitting lid is helpful, but if you don't have one, use a double layer of plastic wrap and aluminum foil.

QUICK CUCUMBER KIMCHI

KOREAN

Makes: 2 cups | **Prep time:** 10 minutes, plus 30 minutes salting time | **Curing time:** 12 to 24 hours

8 ounces Persian cucumbers or other small, crisp cucumbers, cut into ⅛-inch-thick coins (3 to 4 cucumbers)

2 teaspoons kosher salt

2 teaspoons minced garlic (2 cloves)

2 teaspoons grated fresh ginger (¾-inch piece)

2 tablespoons rice vinegar

1 teaspoon fish sauce

2 teaspoons sugar

1 teaspoon Korean red pepper powder or flakes

1 teaspoon store-bought (see ingredient tip) or homemade Korean Red Pepper Paste (page 80)

2 tablespoons finely chopped green onions

1 teaspoon sesame oil

1 teaspoon toasted sesame seeds, for garnish

Traditional kimchi doesn't usually use Korean red pepper paste as one of its ingredients, but I add it to this quickie cucumber kimchi. I make this kimchi in small portions. Because it's so easy and quick, it can be made fresh on demand.

1. Toss the cucumbers with the salt in a colander. Set aside in the sink for 30 minutes.

2. Rinse the cucumbers under cold running water and drain them in the colander.

3. In a medium nonreactive bowl, mix together the garlic, ginger, vinegar, fish sauce, sugar, red pepper powder, red pepper paste, and green onions. Toss the cucumbers with the mixture until evenly coated. Cover and refrigerate for 12 to 24 hours before serving. Just before serving, drizzle with the sesame oil and sprinkle with the sesame seeds.

INGREDIENT TIP: If you don't want to make your own, Korean red pepper paste (gochujang) is available in tubs at Asian markets. Look for a brand that doesn't use flavor enhancers (like MSG) or artificial coloring. If you're gluten-free, read the label carefully. Some brands contain wheat and gluten, while others don't.

BITTER GREENS KIMCHI

KOREA

Makes: 1 quart | Prep time: 20 minutes, plus 8 to 12 hours salting time | Fermenting time: 2 to 6 days

FOR THE GREENS

1½ to 2 pounds bitter greens, like mustard, dandelion, or kale (3 bunches)

3 tablespoons coarse sea salt or kosher salt

3 cups warm water

FOR THE KIMCHI PASTE

½ cup water

2 teaspoons sweet rice or rice flour

2 teaspoons sugar, or to taste (optional)

1 tablespoon minced garlic (3 cloves)

2 teaspoons minced fresh ginger (¼ ounce)

1 tablespoon fish sauce

4 to 6 tablespoons Korean red pepper flakes, depending on taste

1 cup shredded carrot (2 ounces)

½ cup sliced onion (1 small onion)

Salting or brining the vegetables before mixing with the kimchi paste helps preserve the vegetables and allows the kimchi paste to penetrate the vegetables. Which method you use is a matter of preference, but in general brining is better for vegetables with a lower water content.

1. Wash all your equipment in hot, soapy water.

2. PREP THE GREENS: Trim any woody, fibrous, or browned stems and cut the greens into 1-inch pieces. In a large nonreactive bowl, mix together the salt and water until the salt dissolves completely. Add the greens and weigh them down with a heavy plate. They won't be entirely submerged, but they will eventually shrink. Soak for 8 to 12 hours, until wilted.

3. Drain the greens and rinse under cold running water. Drain in a colander while you prepare the kimchi paste.

4. PREP THE PASTE: In a small heatproof bowl, mix together the water and sweet rice flour. Microwave on high for 20 seconds. Stir to remove any lumps. Microwave for 20 more seconds and stir until the mixture thickens. Stir in the sugar (if using) until it dissolves completely.

5. Wearing a pair of food-safe gloves, in a large nonreactive bowl, mix together the rice porridge, garlic, ginger, fish sauce, and red pepper flakes to make the kimchi paste. Add the carrot and onion. Taste and adjust the seasonings if desired. The paste should taste spicy, a little too salty to eat on its own, and a little sweet if you like.

6. Toss the greens with the kimchi paste until they are evenly coated. Pack the greens tightly into 2 pint-size jars, leaving 2 inches of headspace. Rinse the bowl with a little water (2 tablespoons) and pour this liquid into the jars. Push down firmly with your hands to remove any air bubbles. Place a weight (see page 14 for options) on top of the vegetables to keep them submerged under the brine.

7. Wrap the mouth of each jar with plastic wrap and ferment at room temperature away from direct sunlight for 2 to 6 days. The greens will be quite bitter at first, but allow them to ferment for a few days and the bitterness will mellow. The kimchi will release liquid as it ferments, so place the jars on plates to catch any spills.

8. Once the kimchi is fermented to your liking, remove the weights, cap the jars, and store in the refrigerator. (I keep the plastic wrap on to prevent smells from leaking out.) The kimchi will continue to ferment slowly and will keep for up to 1 month.

INGREDIENT TIP: Sweet rice flour is also known by its Japanese name, mochiko or mochi flour. You can find it at Asian markets, and the Koda brand is sold in the international aisle of many supermarkets. If you can't find sweet rice flour, you can use rice flour or all-purpose flour as well.

FERMENTED YELLOW RADISH | TAKUAN

JAPANESE

Makes: 2 quarts | Prep and Cook time: 30 minutes, plus 2 hours drying time, plus 24 hours salting time | Fermenting time: 8 to 14 days

2 to 2½ pounds daikon radish
   (3 large daikon radishes)
¼ cup coarse sea salt or
   kosher salt
3 teaspoons ground turmeric
3 tablespoons sugar

Takuan is one of the most popular Japanese pickles. It is commonly found in bento boxes as garnish or rolled into sushi. The original process for making takuan takes several months. The first step is to dry the daikon radish for several weeks until it is dehydrated and pliable. The daikon is then salted and fermented for months. To shorten the process, I oven-dry the daikon and ferment it for about 10 days. Takuan is traditionally colored with persimmon oranges. To get the same golden hue of authentic takuan, or at least a close approximation, I use turmeric.

1. Wash all your equipment with hot, soapy water. Preheat the oven to 200°F.

2. Peel the daikon and cut it into ⅛-inch-thick full and/or half-moons. Use a mandoline if you have one. Arrange the slices in one layer on two large baking sheets and oven-dry for about 2 hours, until soft and bendable.

3. Wearing food-safe gloves, in a large mixing bowl, toss the daikon, salt, turmeric, and sugar and massage until liquid releases from the daikon slices.

4. Cover the bowl with a large sheet of plastic wrap. Press down firmly on top of the sliced daikon, removing as much air as possible. Place a weight on top of the daikon (I use a heavy plate), cover with a kitchen towel, and set aside at room temperature for 24 hours.

5. Pack the daikon into a half-gallon jar and pour all the juices from the bowl into the jar. Press down firmly using your fingers or a wooden spoon to remove any air pockets and to allow the juices to rise up. If the daikon is not submerged, pour in some water, leaving

at least 2 inches of headspace. Place a weight (see page 14 for options) on top of the daikon to keep it submerged under the brine. Place the jar on a plate to catch any spills.

6. Cap the jar loosely and ferment at room temperature away from direct sunlight for 8 to 14 days. Burp daily for the first few days to release pressure from the carbon dioxide that forms.

7. After 5 days, start tasting the takuan every day. Once the takuan is fermented to your liking, cap the jar tightly and store in the refrigerator. It will continue to ferment slowly and will keep for 6 months.

INGREDIENT TIP: You can cut the daikon any way you like: long flat cuts for sandwiches, thin rounds for eating with your fingers, or long sticks (¼- to ½-inch width/height and about 6 inches long) for sushi rolls. You may have to adjust the oven-drying time.

SALTED RICE KOJI PICKLES | SHIO KOJI ASAZUKE

JAPAN

Makes: 1½ cups or 1 pound of shio koji (enough for about 10 pounds of pickles) |
Prep time: 10 minutes, plus 2 to 3 hours mixing time | **Shio Koji Fermenting time:** 1 to 2 weeks |
Vegetable Fermenting time: 20 minutes to 24 hours

FOR THE PICKLING MEDIUM

1⅓ cups water

¼ cup coarse sea salt or kosher salt

1 (7-ounce) package prepared rice koji

FOR THE PICKLES

1 pound of any of the following vegetables:

Carrots, peeled and cut on the diagonal

Daikon radish, peeled and cut into sticks

Bell peppers, seeded and quartered

Green beans, trimmed

Broccoli, cut into florets

Shio koji, or salt koji, is a pickling medium made by salting and soaking rice koji, which is cooked rice that has been inoculated with koji, a naturally occurring culture that's everywhere in Japan. The final product looks like rice porridge. Foods like soy sauce, miso, and mirin are also fermented using koji. The enzymes in koji break down proteins into amino acids that turn into glutamate, or what we know as umami. You can buy ready-made shio koji, but it is usually heat-treated, which negates its beneficial probiotic properties. In this recipe, I show you how to make shio koji from rice koji, which is sold at Japanese markets and online.

Once the shio koji is fermented, you're ready to pickle vegetables. The general rule for how much shio koji you need to ferment vegetables is 1:10, or 10 percent of the weight of your vegetables. This recipe makes 1 pound of shio koji, which can pickle about 10 pounds of vegetables. I usually use whatever I need to cover the vegetables, keeping in mind that it's quite salty. Keep experimenting and you'll find the optimum pickling time and amounts.

1. Wash all your equipment in hot, soapy water.

2. MAKE THE PICKLING MEDIUM: In a large glass measuring cup or heatproof bowl, bring the water to a boil in the microwave (it will take 2 to 3 minutes, depending on your microwave), or use a medium saucepan on the stove top. Stir the salt into the water until it dissolves completely. Set aside to cool to 140°F.

3. Meanwhile, wash your hands thoroughly. Break up the koji with your fingers, add it to the water at 140°F, and mix well. Mix every so often for the next 2 to 3 hours.

4. Transfer the mixture to a quart-size or larger container with a tight-fitting lid. You want to be able to stir the shio koji without spilling it. Cover and ferment at room temperature away from direct sunlight.

5. Mix the shio koji once a day for at least 1 week (summer) and up to to 2 weeks (winter). You may need to add water on the second day if all the water has been absorbed. Just add enough to cover.

6. Taste the shio koji now and then; it should be sweet and salty with a pleasant smell. It will be too salty at the beginning, but fermentation will sweeten it. Once you taste this sweetness, store the shio koji in the refrigerator. Shio koji will keep in the refrigerator for 6 to 10 months.

7. MAKE THE PICKLES: When you're ready to pickle, peel and cut 1 pound of vegetables into bite-size pieces with the largest surface area possible. For example, cut carrots and cucumbers into diagonal pieces. Blanch vegetables you don't normally eat raw, like green beans or asparagus. Salt vegetables with a high water content, like daikon, to remove moisture.

8. Put the cut vegetables in a shallow dish with a lid (you can use plastic wrap) or a zip-top bag. Add about ¼ cup (1.6 ounces) shio koji and massage into the vegetables. Ferment in the refrigerator for 20 minutes or up to 24 hours. Softer vegetables like cucumbers and bell peppers will be quick (20 minutes), and green beans will need 2 to 3 hours, while carrots and turnips may take 1 day or even longer. Taste every so often to see how you like the pickles.

9. Rinse the shio koji off of the vegetables before eating. Once pickled, they will keep for 1 or 2 days in the refrigerator.

SHAN PICKLES | MON-NYIN CHIN

MYANMAR

Makes: 1 pint | **Prep time:** 20 minutes, plus 10 to 15 minutes sitting time | **Fermenting time:** 3 days

½ pound bitter greens like
  bok choy, Swiss chard, or
  mustard cabbage

3 cups carrots, sliced
  thin on the diagonal
  (3 medium carrots)

½ cup small shallots or
  pickling red onions, peeled
  (¼ pound)

1 tablespoon coarse sea salt or
  kosher salt

1 tablespoon brown sugar

1 tablespoon paprika

2 teaspoons dried chili flakes,
  or to taste

1 teaspoon ground turmeric

1 cup lager or any other
  light beer

This is a popular Burmese pickle traditionally made by the Shan people, hence its name. It literally means "sour mustard greens" but generally refers to all kinds of pickles. The classic Shan pickle is composed of mustard greens, carrots, leek bulbs, garlic chive roots, and/or Chinese artichokes. Other commonly used vegetables include elephant garlic, radish stems, cabbage, cauliflower, bean sprouts, green mango, and bamboo shoots. But don't worry, I'm not going to make you hunt down obscure vegetables. Here, I have adapted a recipe I found in *Under the Golden Pagoda: The Best of Burmese Cooking* by Aung Aung Taik. I believe the beer must be a substitute for rice wine, which was hard to come by in the United States at the time. I think it gives the pickle a distinct flavor, but feel free to substitute ¼ cup Chinese rice wine plus ¾ cup water.

1. Wash all your equipment in hot, soapy water.

2. Bring a large kettle of water to a boil.

3. Rinse the greens leaf by leaf to remove any dirt, especially near the bottom of the stems. Put them in a large heatproof bowl and pour in boiling water to cover. Set aside for 10 to 15 minutes, until wilted. Drain the greens in a colander and dry with kitchen towels. Cut them into ¼-inch-wide pieces.

4. Wearing a pair of food-safe gloves, in a large nonreactive bowl, toss together the greens, carrots, shallots, salt, sugar, paprika, chili flakes, and turmeric. Massage for 10 minutes to infuse the spices into the vegetables. Pour in the beer and mix again. Taste and adjust the seasonings if desired.

5. Place a heavy plate or other weight (see page 14 for options) on top of the vegetables to keep them submerged under the brine. Cover the bowl with plastic wrap and ferment at room temperature away from direct sunlight for at least 3 days. Once the pickle is fermented to your liking, pack into a pint-size jar, pushing down to remove any air bubbles. Cap the jar and store in the refrigerator. It will continue to ferment slowly and will keep for 1 to 2 months.

SALT-PICKLED MUSTARD CABBAGE | SUAN CAI

CHINA/TAIWAN

Makes: 2 quarts | Prep time: 10 minutes, plus 1 to 2 hours salting time |
Fermenting time: 5 to 10 days

1½ to 2 pounds Chinese
    mustard cabbage, trimmed
    and halved (1 large cabbage)
¼ cup coarse sea salt
    or kosher salt, plus
    2 tablespoons
4 cups water

Pickled mustard cabbage is a staple in Chinese-influenced cuisine. I love the dish for its pucker power and its crunchy stems. Called suan cai (literally sour vegetable), zha cai, or kiam chye, this popular condiment accompanies Taiwanese beef noodles and Thai red curry chicken noodles (khao soi). You can buy them at the Asian market, but ever since I started to ferment my own, I've never gone back to store-bought. Pick a mature cabbage with not as much water content.

1. Wash all your equipment in hot, soapy water.

2. In a large nonreactive bowl, sprinkle the cabbage with 2 tablespoons of salt. Massage the salt into the cabbage, making sure to get in between the stems and leaves, especially near the core. Set aside for 1 to 2 hours at room temperature, massaging and tossing every once in a while. When the leaves are wilted, rinse the cabbage under cold running water to remove any excess salt and dirt. Shake and drain in a colander.

3. Meanwhile, combine the remaining ¼ cup of salt and the water in a medium saucepan over medium-high heat. Bring to a boil and stir until the salt dissolves completely.

4. Cut the cabbage into large pieces if desired and pack into a 2-quart jar. Pour in the brine, leaving 2 inches of headspace. Place a weight (see page 14 for options) on top of the cabbage to keep it submerged under the brine. Place the jar on a small plate to catch any spills.

5. Cap the jar loosely and ferment at room temperature away from direct sunlight for 5 days (in summer) to 10 days (in winter), until salty and slightly sour. The cabbage will turn a bright yellowish green. Burp daily for the first few days to release pressure from the carbon dioxide that forms.

6. Taste the cabbage every few days. Once the cabbage is fermented to your liking, store it in the refrigerator. It will continue to ferment slowly and will keep for 6 months.

   SWITCH IT UP: Pickle bok choy or Chinese (napa) cabbage using this same method for a different taste and texture.

SICHUAN PICKLES | PAO CAI

CHINA

Makes: 1 quart | **Prep and Cook time:** 30 minutes | **Fermenting time:** 1 day to 1 month

3 cups water

3 tablespoons coarse sea salt
  or kosher salt

1 tablespoon sugar

2 tablespoons Chinese cooking
  wine or dry sherry (gin or
  vodka work, too)

1½ pounds assorted
  vegetables, such as
  cabbage, radish, carrot,
  celery, cauliflower, fresh
  chile peppers, etc., cut into
  bite-size pieces

2 garlic cloves, smashed

1 (1-inch) piece fresh ginger,
  peeled and cut into 3 or
  4 slices

1 star anise pod (optional)

1 teaspoon Sichuan
  peppercorns (optional)

½ teaspoon fennel
  seeds (optional)

2 small dried red chiles, like
  chiles de arbol (optional)

Pickled vegetables are essential to Sichuanese cookery. Many households have a pao cai tan zi, a rough earthenware pot housing a stash of pickles in a pool of brine. New vegetables are added every few days, but the pickling brine, or the "mother liquor," is used indefinitely.

1. Wash all your equipment with hot, soapy water.

2. Bring the water to a boil in a medium saucepan, then add the salt and sugar. Stir until they dissolve completely. Set aside to cool to room temperature and add the Chinese wine. Taste the brine and adjust the seasonings if desired.

3. Pack the assorted vegetables into a quart-size jar. Slip in the garlic, ginger, and any or all of the optional ingredients: star anise, Sichuan peppercorns, fennel seeds, and dried chiles.

4. Pour in the brine, leaving 1 inch of headspace. You may not use all of it. Place a weight on top of the vegetables (see page 14 for options) to keep them submerged under the brine. Cap the jar loosely and ferment at room temperature away from direct sunlight for up to 1 month. Set the jar on a plate to catch any spills. Burp daily for the first few days to release pressure from the carbon dioxide that forms.

5. Start tasting after 1 day (summer) or 2 days (winter). Once the vegetables are fermented to your liking, store in the refrigerator. The pickles will continue to ferment slowly and will keep for 6 months.

INGREDIENT TIP: To reuse the pickling brine, add 2 teaspoons of salt and a splash of Chinese wine to the brine every time you add new vegetables. Replace the spices every month or so.

DAIKON AND JICAMA WATER KIMCHI | DONGCHIMI

KOREA

Makes: 1 quart | **Prep and Cook time:** 30 minutes, plus 24 hours salting time | **Fermenting time:** 1 to 2 days

½ pound daikon radish, peeled and cut into 1-inch cubes

½ pound jicama, peeled and cut into 1-inch cubes

2 tablespoons coarse sea salt or kosher salt, divided

1 tablespoon sugar, plus 2 teaspoons

3 cups water

2 garlic cloves, smashed and peeled

1 (½-inch) piece fresh ginger, cut into 3 or 4 slices

4 green onions, cut into 2-inch pieces

Dongchimi is a refreshing summer kimchi that's popular as a side dish or cold soup. It's not what most non-Koreans expect from a typical kimchi. It is traditionally prepared with just daikon radish, but I've paired the daikon with sweet jicama in this version. Tart rather than spicy, dongchimi falls under the "white" or "water" kimchi (mul kimchi) category. This pickle is very easy to make and requires only a brief fermentation period.

1. Wash all your equipment with hot, soapy water.

2. Toss the daikon and jicama with 1 tablespoon salt and 2 teaspoons of sugar. Cover and set aside for 24 hours at room temperature.

3. Rinse the daikon and jicama under cold running water and drain in a colander.

4. Combine the remaining 1 tablespoon salt, the remaining 1 tablespoon sugar, and the water in a small saucepan over medium heat. Bring to a boil and stir until the salt and sugar dissolve completely. Set aside to cool.

5. In a quart-size jar, combine the daikon, jicama, garlic, ginger, and green onions. Cover and ferment for 1 to 2 days at room temperature, until the broth tastes a little vinegary. Pour the cooled brine over the vegetables. Then store it in the refrigerator, where it will keep for up to 1 week.

TRY IT WITH: You can also serve this dish without fermenting. To mimic the tart fermented flavor, add 3 tablespoons of vinegar before serving. To serve, ladle the vegetables and a few scoops of broth into a cup or small bowl.

RED VEGETABLE KIMCHI

KOREA
Makes: 1 pint | **Prep time:** 20 minutes, plus 12 to 24 hours salting time | **Fermenting time:** 3 to 10 days

½ pound beets, any variety
    (2 medium beets)
4 cups water
¼ cup coarse sea salt or
    kosher salt
½ pound red cabbage,
    cut into 1-inch squares
    (½ small cabbage)
1 tablespoon minced garlic
1 tablespoon minced
    fresh ginger
1 tablespoon fish sauce
2 teaspoons sugar (optional)
¼ to ½ cup Korean red
    pepper flakes (gochujaru),
    depending on taste
4 green onions, cut into
    1-inch pieces

I love beets: red beets, golden beets, and Chioggia beets (which are red-and-white striped). Every fall and winter, I'm inundated with an assortment in my CSA box, and I'm always looking for new ways to prepare them. Last winter, I decided to kimchi-fy them! I chose to pair red beets and red cabbage because they are similar in color and, being sturdy vegetables, would ferment at the same rate. You can feel free to mix any-colored beets with any vegetable, including daikon radish, Chinese (napa) cabbage, or carrots, but then it wouldn't be called Red Vegetable Kimchi anymore!

1. Wash all your equipment with hot, soapy water.

2. Peel or scrub the beets. Halve or quarter them and cut them into ⅛-inch-thick slices.

3. Bring the water to a boil in a medium saucepan over medium-high heat. Then add the salt and stir until it dissolves completely. Allow the brine to cool to room temperature.

4. Combine the beets, cabbage, and brine in a large nonreactive bowl and soak for 12 to 24 hours, until the beets are soft and bendable.

5. Drain the vegetables in a colander and rinse under cold running water.

6. Wearing a pair of food-safe gloves, in a large nonreactive bowl, mix together the garlic, ginger, fish sauce, sugar (if using), and red pepper flakes to make the kimchi paste. Add a little water if the paste is too dry. Add the green onions. Taste and adjust the seasonings if desired. The paste should taste spicy, a little too salty to eat on its own, and a little sweet if you like.

7. Toss the beets and cabbage with the kimchi paste. Pack them into a pint-size jar, leaving 2 inches of headspace. Rinse the bowl with a little water (2 tablespoons) and pour this liquid into the jar. Push down firmly with your hands to remove any air bubbles. Place a weight (see page 14 for options) on top of the vegetables to keep them submerged under the brine. Wrap the mouth of the jar with plastic wrap and ferment at room temperature away from direct sunlight for 3 to 10 days. The kimchi will release liquid as it ferments, so place the jar on a plate to catch any spills.

8. Once the kimchi is fermented to your liking, cap the jar and store in the refrigerator. (I keep the plastic wrap on to prevent smells from leaking out.) The kimchi will continue to ferment slowly and will keep for up to 1 month.

   PREP TIP: The vegetables will continue to release liquid during fermentation, so don't worry if they aren't completely submerged at first. Additionally, the salting and the red pepper flakes add to the kimchi's preservative power. If the vegetables are not fully submerged by the second day, you can make a brine using 1 cup water and 1 tablespoon salt and pour it into the jar.

MISO-GINGER SAUERKRAUT

JAPANESE-GERMAN FUSION

Makes: 2 quarts | Prep time: 30 minutes, plus 1 hour salting time |
Fermenting time: 3 days to 1 month

1½ to 2 pounds Savoy or
green cabbage, shredded
(1 medium cabbage)

4 teaspoons coarse sea salt or
kosher salt

2 tablespoons mild white miso

¼ cup boiling water

4 teaspoons minced
fresh ginger

1 tablespoon minced garlic
(3 cloves)

2 cups shredded carrots
(4 ounces)

2 green onions, chopped

Even though sauerkraut is more of a European pickling tradition, its principles are similar to those of kimchi-making. Salt the vegetables, then ferment with spices submerged in brine and let the magic happen. That magic, of course, is lactofermentation. This process allows beneficial lactobacillus bacteria to convert sugars into lactic acid and promotes a healthier digestive system. I've added miso and ginger to give this kraut some Japanese flair. Keep in mind that fermented vegetables like sauerkraut generally do well with 2 to 3 percent salt by weight or 4 to 5 teaspoons of coarse sea salt per pound. Start with less and adjust to taste right before you pack the cabbage into jars. It's easier to add salt than to take it away.

1. Wash all your equipment with hot, soapy water.

2. Toss the cabbage and salt together in a large nonreactive bowl. Massage and squeeze the cabbage with clean hands for several minutes, until the cabbage is soft and begins to release its juices. The cabbage is ready if when you pick up a handful and squeeze, juices drip down just as water releases from a wet sponge. Cover with a kitchen towel and set aside for 1 hour.

3. Meanwhile, whisk the miso into the boiling water in a second large nonreactive bowl. Set aside to cool. When it is cool, mix in the ginger, garlic, carrots, and green onions.

4. After the cabbage has sat for 1 hour, massage the miso mixture into the cabbage until evenly coated. Taste and add more seasonings if desired. Pack the cabbage into 2 quart-size jars or 1 half-gallon jar. Press down firmly using your fingers or a wooden spoon to remove any air pockets and to allow the juices to rise up. Leave about 2 inches of headspace. Place a weight

(see page 14 for options) on top of the cabbage to submerge as much as possible under the brine. The kraut will continue to release juices, so place the jar(s) on a small plate to catch any spills.

5. Cap the jar(s) loosely and keep at room temperature and away from direct sunlight for anywhere from 3 days to 1 month. Burp daily for the first few days to release pressure from the carbon dioxide that forms. After 36 hours, if the kraut isn't completely submerged in brine, stir together 1 tablespoon salt and 1 cup water and add as much of this brine as necessary.

6. Taste the sauerkraut every few days. Once the kraut is fermented to your liking, cap the jar(s) tightly and store in the refrigerator. The kraut will continue to ferment slowly and will keep for months.

INGREDIENT TIP: For this recipe, you can use any type of miso you have on hand. Darker misos (like a red miso) will be saltier, so you may want to start with less salt and/or add more sugar.

FERMENTED EGGPLANT | CA PHAO MUOI

VIETNAM

Makes: 1 quart | Prep time: 10 minutes, plus 1 hour salting time | Fermenting time: 3 to 7 days

1 pound Asian eggplant
  (2 small eggplants)
3 to 4 tablespoons coarse sea
  salt or kosher salt, divided
2 cups water
2 pieces galangal, sliced into
  ¼-inch-thick pieces
2 garlic cloves

Vietnamese-style pickled eggplant is usually made with round, golf-ball-size white eggplants. Here, I've sliced easier-to-find thin-skinned eggplants into strips and fermented them in brine for a similar pickle. Eat this pickle out of the jar or with any rice dish as a delicious condiment.

1. Wash all your equipment in hot, soapy water.

2. Cut the eggplant crosswise into ¼-inch-thick discs. Place the discs in a colander over the sink and sprinkle with 1 to 2 tablespoons of salt. Gently massage the salt into the eggplant. Cover and set aside for at least 1 hour to remove moisture and soften the eggplant.

3. Rinse the eggplant under cold running water and drain in a colander.

4. In a small saucepan over medium-high heat, bring the water to a boil. Stir in the remaining 2 tablespoons of salt until it dissolves completely. Set aside to cool completely.

5. Slip 1 slice galangal and 1 garlic clove into a quart-size jar. Pack the eggplant into the jar, squishing them as you go. Slip the remaining slice of galangal and the remaining garlic clove on top. Pour in the brine, leaving 2 inches of headspace. Place a weight (see page 14 for options) on top of the eggplant to keep it submerged under the brine.

6. Cap the jar loosely with a lid and ferment at room temperature away from direct sunlight for 3 to 7 days. Burp daily for the first few days to release pressure from the carbon dioxide that forms.

7. Once the eggplant is fermented to your liking, store in the refrigerator. It will keep for several months.

   INGREDIENT TIP: Asian eggplants, which include Japanese eggplants and Chinese eggplants, have thinner skins and a more delicate flavor than American globe eggplants. Italian eggplants and heirloom fairy tale eggplants are similar to the Asian varieties. If you can only find globe eggplants, peel the skin and cut the flesh into strips. If you notice the garlic turning blue or green in your pickling brine, don't panic. It's still safe to eat. This color change is caused by a chemical reaction that occurs with the acid in the brine, depending on the age of the garlic, the temperature, and the pH.

CHAPTER 5

Pickling Outside the Box

Apple and Celery Kimchi 122

Asian Pear and Fennel Pickles 124

Pickled Chickpeas, Two Ways 126

Spiced Chickpea Pickle 127

Soy Sauce–Pickled Eggs | Shoyu Tamago 128

Pickled Shallots 129

Pickled Tea Leaf Dressing | Laphet Thoke 130

Soy-Pickled Bitter Melon 132

Citrus Chile Paste | Yuzu Kosho 133

Chili Oil 134

Spicy Bamboo Shoots in Chili Oil 135

Salt-Cured Eggs 136

Pickled Sunchokes 138

Pickled Chayote 140

Pickled Peanuts | Lao Cu Huasheng 141

Salty Limeade | Chanh Muõi 142

Pickled Sweet Potatoes 143

Chinese Five-Spice Pickled Grapes 144

Seven Gods Curry Pickle | Fukujinzuke 146

PICKLE PASSPORT: CHINA

Must-try pickles: Salt-Pickled Mustard Cabbage (page 108),
Spicy Smacked Cucumbers (page 38), Sichuan Pickles (page 110),
Quick Cucumber and Carrot Pickles (page 27)

China has a long history of pickling, dating back to the Zhou Dynasty in 1100 BCE, and the Chinese people have always valued fermented foods for their health benefits. In fact, methods of pickling in other regions, such as Korean kimchi and German sauerkraut, are believed to have been inspired by practices originating in China.

Like many other cultures, the Chinese pickled vegetables during the harvest season to be consumed throughout the year. Additionally, the origin stories of many regional fermented delicacies reflect extreme poverty and describe accidental discoveries that transformed spoiled, inedible, or overlooked odds and ends into delicious foods through fermentation.

There is no one "Chinese pickle." Northern and Southern styles are very different, and every province, town, and village boasts its own style of pickle or ferment. Broadly, however, there are two main styles of pickling in China. One style uses a wet or dry brine and various spices to pickle vegetables for a few hours or over a longer period of time. This is called "xian cai" or salty vegetables. This method includes lactofermented vegetables. One of the most popular Chinese ferments is Salt-Pickled Mustard Cabbage (page 108), a traditional Chinese pickle that is enjoyed throughout the country. Sichuan Pickles (page 110) are another popular lactoferment that is unique to Sichuan province.

The second style is "jiang cai," or sauce vegetables. This version uses soy sauce or savory bean sauce as a pickling base. Sugar is added for a salty-sweet taste.

Just as Chinese cuisine is composed of an assortment of flavors, Chinese pickles are often enhanced by a variety of flavors, set off by Sichuan peppers, soy sauce, chili oil, star anise, fennel seeds, and many more ingredients. These flavors aim to strike a balance of sweet, salty, bitter, sour, pungent, and spicy notes using a combination of ingredients and the vegetables or fruits being pickled.

In China, pickles are often cooked into a dish, such as in Teochew-style duck and salted mustard cabbage soup. They are also eaten as an appetizer with beer or tea to stimulate the appetite or served as a palate cleanser at the end of a meal.

APPLE AND CELERY KIMCHI

KOREA

Makes: 2 quarts | **Prep time:** 20 minutes, plus 30 minutes salting time | **Fermenting time:** 8 hours

1 tablespoon coarse sea salt or kosher salt

2¼ cups water, divided

1½ pounds crisp, sweet-tart apples like Pink Lady, Granny Smith, or Fuji, cored and chopped (3 apples)

1 cup chopped celery stalks (2 celery stalks)

2 teaspoons sweet rice flour

1 tablespoon sugar (optional)

1 tablespoon white miso

1 tablespoon minced garlic (3 cloves)

1 tablespoon minced fresh ginger (⅓ ounce)

2 to 4 tablespoons Korean red pepper flakes (gochujaru), depending on taste

½ cup sliced onion (½ medium onion)

For this recipe, I decided it was time to make apples the star of the show. Then I wondered whether, instead of fish sauce or fermented shrimp, I could use other umami-packed seasonings. I'd seen soy sauce used, so here I decided to try miso. The resulting kimchi is delightful, a little spicy, a little sweet and tart, with a hint of umami waiting in the wings.

1. Wash all your equipment in hot, soapy water.

2. Mix together the salt and 2 cups water in a large nonreactive bowl, until the salt dissolves completely. Add the apple and celery and soak for 30 minutes to prevent browning.

3. Drain the apple and celery in a colander and rinse under cold running water.

4. Meanwhile, mix together the remaining ¼ cup of water and the sweet rice flour in a small heatproof bowl. Microwave on high for 20 seconds. Stir to remove any lumps. Microwave for 20 more seconds and stir until the mixture thickens. Stir in the sugar (if using) until it dissolves completely. Stir in the miso.

5. Wearing a pair of food-safe gloves, mix together the rice porridge mixture, garlic, ginger, and red pepper flakes in a separate large nonreactive bowl to make the kimchi paste. Add the onion. Taste and adjust the seasonings if desired. The paste should taste spicy, a little too salty to eat on its own, and a little sweet if you like.

6. Toss the apple and celery in the kimchi paste until well coated. The kimchi is ready to eat immediately, but I like to leave it at room temperature for 8 hours and then store it in the refrigerator. I don't recommend keeping apple kimchi for longer than 2 to 3 days. The kimchi flavors will eventually overpower the apple.

INGREDIENT TIP: I like to use a mix of apples in this kimchi to get varying flavors and textures. I don't peel them, but please do so if you prefer!

ASIAN-WESTERN FUSION

Makes: 2 quarts | **Prep and Cook time:** 20 minutes | **Curing time:** 4 days

2 pounds Asian pears, or any other sweet, firm pear (3 to 4 pears)

1 teaspoon lemon juice mixed into 4 cups water

1 (8-ounce) fennel bulb, cored and cut into thin slices

6 (2-inch) pieces orange zest

1 cup apple cider vinegar

½ cup distilled white vinegar

¾ cup water

1½ cups sugar

½ teaspoon coarse sea salt or kosher salt

3 to 4 tablespoons freshly squeezed orange juice (from 1 small orange)

Asian pears (sometimes called apple pears) have tan-brown skin with creamy, white flesh that is crisp and grainy in texture. Sweet and fragrant, they have a high water content and tend to bruise easily. That's why you will often find them wrapped in foam at the store. Select pears that are firm and unblemished.

1. Wash all your equipment with hot, soapy water.

2. Peel the pears, cut them into quarters or eighths, and core them. As you cut, drop the pear slices into the lemon water to prevent them from browning.

3. Divide the fennel and orange zest between 2 quart-size jars.

4. Bring the apple cider vinegar, white vinegar, water, sugar, salt, and orange juice to a boil in a medium nonreactive saucepan. Reduce the heat to a simmer.

5. Tip the pears into the saucepan and simmer for 5 minutes, until they turn white and are just cooked through but still firm. The pears should pierce easily with a fork but shouldn't be mushy. Remove from the heat. Transfer the pears to the jars with a slotted spoon, packing them in tightly. Leave at least 1 inch of headspace.

6. Pour the brine into the jars to cover the pears and fennel completely. Cap the jars immediately and set aside at room temperature and away from direct sunlight for 1 day before storing in the refrigerator. The pears and fennel are ready to eat after 3 days in the refrigerator. They will keep in the refrigerator for 1 month, but the color will begin to change after 2 weeks.

YES YOU CAN! This pear and fennel pickle can be canned so it keeps for up to 1 year on the shelf. Feel free to double or triple the recipe. Following the canning instructions on page 15, place the hot pears and fennel in hot jars that have been washed with hot, soapy water. Fill the jars with hot brine, leaving a ½-inch headspace. Remove any air bubbles, wipe the rims, and seal the jars. Process in a water-bath canner for 20 minutes (pints) or 25 minutes (quarts). Wait 5 minutes before removing the jars, and check the seals after 12 to 24 hours.

HONEY-PICKLED CHICKPEAS

INDIAN-INSPIRED

Makes: 2 cups | **Prep and Cook time:** 10 minutes | **Pickling time:** 24 hours

½ cup apple cider vinegar

2 tablespoons sugar

1 tablespoon honey

¼ teaspoon salt

½ teaspoon cumin seeds

1 (1-inch) cinnamon stick

¼ teaspoon Sichuan or
   black peppercorns

2 cups cooked chickpeas or
   1 (15½-ounce) can, drained
   and rinsed

1 garlic clove, sliced

1 Thai red chile, chopped, or
   to taste

Chickpeas, also called garbanzo beans, are the star ingredient in hummus. While I've eaten chickpeas roasted as a snack and braised in curries, I would never have thought of pickling chickpeas if my editor hadn't suggested it. But why not? Enjoy these pickled chickpeas as a topping for green and pasta salads, or add them as protein to your rice bowl.

1. In a medium saucepan over medium heat, combine the vinegar, sugar, honey, and salt. Stir until the sugar, honey, and salt dissolve. Remove from the heat.

2. In a small skillet over medium heat, dry roast the cumin, cinnamon, and peppercorns until they start to pop and release their fragrance, 2 to 3 minutes. Watch carefully so the spices don't burn. Remove from the heat and pour the spices into the hot brine.

3. Put the chickpeas in a pint-size jar or glass container. Slip in the garlic and chile. Pour the brine over the chickpeas and top off with water, if necessary, to cover them completely. Cap tightly and shake to mix the water with the brine. Refrigerate for at least 24 hours. The pickled chickpeas will keep in the refrigerator for up to 3 weeks.

SPICED CHICKPEA PICKLE

INDIA

Makes: 2 cups | **Prep and Cook time:** 20 minutes | **Pickling time:** 3 weeks

2 cups cooked chickpeas or
  1 (15½-ounce) can, drained
  and rinsed

1 teaspoon red chili powder,
  like cayenne

¼ teaspoon ground turmeric

1 teaspoon salt (or to taste)

1 teaspoon mustard seeds

½ teaspoon fenugreek seeds

2 or 3 curry leaves (optional)

¼ cup vegetable oil, like
  canola or sunflower

1 tablespoon sesame oil

1 teaspoon mango powder
  (amchur) or lime juice

Combining mangos and chickpeas in a traditional Indian pickle is not uncommon. However, when mangos aren't easy to come by, you can make this pickle with chickpeas alone. This chickpea pickle is delicious eaten with rice and yogurt, and as a bonus, chickpeas are an excellent source of vegan protein. For more information on mango powder, check out the tip in the Tomato-Date Chutney recipe on page 64.

1. Wash all your equipment with hot, soapy water.

2. In a medium nonreactive bowl, toss the chickpeas with the chili powder, turmeric, and salt. Set aside.

3. In a small skillet over medium heat, dry roast the mustard seeds, fenugreek seeds, and curry leaves (if using) until they start to pop and release their fragrance, 1 to 2 minutes. Watch carefully so the spices don't burn. Remove from the heat and set aside to cool. Grind to a fine powder with a mortar and pestle or a spice grinder.

4. Using the same skillet over medium heat, warm the vegetable oil until hot but not smoking. Pour over the spice mixture and set aside to cool.

5. When the spice-flavored oil is cool, pour it over the chickpeas and gently mix until the chickpeas are covered evenly. Add the sesame oil and mango powder and gently mix. Transfer the pickle to a pint-size glass jar. Cap tightly and keep at room temperature away from direct sunlight for 1 week, shaking the jar or stirring daily. The pickle will be ready in 3 weeks. Store the pickle in the refrigerator, and it will keep for up to 6 months.

SOY SAUCE-PICKLED EGGS | SHOYU TAMAGO

JAPAN

Makes: 6 eggs | Prep time: 20 minutes | Cook time: 6 minutes | Pickling time: 4 to 24 hours

2 quarts water, plus ½ cup
6 large eggs
½ cup soy sauce
¼ cup mirin
2 tablespoons rice vinegar
¼ cup sugar

Soy sauce-pickled eggs are easy to make yet packed with umami. Some recipes add sake and kombu (dried kelp) to the mix, while others have only two ingredients, soy sauce and mirin. If you're feeling fancy, add some spices, perhaps star anise, shichimi togarashi (7-spice blend), or cumin.

1. In a large saucepan, bring 2 quarts of water to a boil. Gently drop the eggs into the saucepan straight from the refrigerator. Adjust the heat so that the water is simmering gently (around 190°F), and simmer the eggs for 6 minutes (longer, if you prefer your eggs firmer). Prepare a bowl of ice water. When the eggs are done, remove them with a slotted spoon and dunk them in the ice water to stop them from cooking further.

2. When the eggs are cool enough to handle, peel them and arrange them so they fit snugly into a nonreactive container. (I use a rectangular 4-cup glass container with a tight-fitting lid.)

3. In a mixing bowl, mix together the soy sauce, mirin, remaining ½ cup of water, rice vinegar, and sugar and stir until the sugar dissolves completely. Pour the brine over the eggs. Place a folded paper towel over the eggs to keep them submerged under the brine for at least 4 hours, or up to 24 hours. The yolks will start to cure if they remain in the brine for too long. Drain the eggs and store in the refrigerator. The eggs will keep for 3 to 4 days.

TRY IT WITH: Soy sauce-pickled eggs make a satisfying midafternoon snack, or eat them as your protein with a bowl of ramen or some rice.

PICKLED SHALLOTS

THAILAND
Makes: 1 quart | Prep time: 15 minutes, plus 8 to 24 hours salting time | Cook time: 15 minutes | Fermenting time: 4 days | Curing time: 1 week

2 tablespoons coarse sea salt or kosher salt, plus 2 teaspoons

2½ cups water, divided

1 pound small shallots, peeled but kept intact

1½ cups distilled white vinegar

½ cup sugar

2 Thai chiles, pricked with a fork

2 Asian lime leaves or strips of lime zest

1 lemongrass bulb, smashed (or 2 lemongrass tops, see page 78)

The overnight brining process draws moisture from the shallots, which helps them maintain their crunch, so don't skip this step. If small Asian shallots are hard to find (they're usually about 1¼ inches long, weigh ½ ounce, and are sold at Asian markets), opt for red pickling onions instead.

1. Wash all your equipment with hot, soapy water.

2. In a large bowl, stir together 2 tablespoons of salt and 2 cups of water, until the salt dissolves. Soak the shallots in the brine for 8 to 24 hours.

3. Drain the shallots, rinse under cold running water, and drain in a colander.

4. Meanwhile, in a small saucepan over medium heat, combine the vinegar, remaining ½ cup of water, sugar, remaining 2 teaspoons of salt, chiles, lime leaves, and lemongrass bulb and bring to a boil. Then adjust the heat and simmer for 5 minutes. Remove from the heat and set aside to cool.

5. Pack the shallots into a quart-size jar and pour in the vinegar brine. Cap the jar and keep in the sun or a warm, dry place for at least 4 days. Taste, and once the shallots are sour enough to your liking, store in the refrigerator for 1 more week before eating. Pickled shallots will keep in the refrigerator for about 6 months.

TRY IT WITH: Pickled shallots will cut through any spicy Thai curry. Or slice them up to top tacos, sandwiches, or burgers.

PICKLED TEA LEAF DRESSING | LAPHET THOKE

MYANMAR

Makes: ⅓ cup | **Prep time:** 10 minutes, plus 10 minutes sitting time | **Fermenting time:** 2 to 3 days | **Curing time:** 3 days

¼ cup good quality loose-leaf green tea, like Sencha

2 garlic cloves

1 (1-inch) piece fresh ginger, peeled

2 small dried red chiles, like chiles de arbol, or 1 teaspoon dried chili flakes

1 teaspoon fish sauce or soy sauce, plus more for the salad

1 tablespoon fresh lime juice

¼ cup vegetable oil, like sunflower or avocado

4 cups chopped Chinese cabbage or romaine lettuce

1½ cups chopped fresh tomatoes

Handful fresh cilantro leaves

3 tablespoons crushed roasted peanuts

3 tablespoons toasted sunflower seeds

1 tablespoon toasted sesame seeds

Sesame oil, for drizzling

I first had pickled tea leaf salad at a San Francisco restaurant called Burma SuperStar. One bite, and I was hooked. Salty pickled tea leaves were mashed to a pulp and mixed with chiles, garlic, and ginger, then tossed with romaine lettuce, tomatoes, fried garlic bits, and roasted nuts and seeds. While fermented tea leaves are sold all over Myanmar, they're not easy to find in the United States. Fortunately, cookbook author Naomi Duguid (author of *Burma: Rivers of Flavor*) introduced me to a version using dried green tea leaves. I've adapted her recipe here.

1. Pick out twigs or hard pieces from the tea leaves.

2. Make the tea by bringing a kettle of water to a boil (use enough water to fill your mug). Place the tea leaves in a tea pot or a large mug. Pour in the freshly boiled water and steep the tea leaves for 10 minutes.

3. Strain the tea liquid and drink it if you want. Press the tea leaves with the back of a spoon to squeeze out excess liquid. Taste the tea leaves. If they are too bitter, steep in boiling water for another 3 to 5 minutes and strain again.

4. Transfer the tea leaves to a small container (I use a glass Pyrex bowl) and cover with a kitchen towel or several layers of cheesecloth. Keep at room temperature and away from direct sunlight for 2 to 3 days, until the tea leaves smell a little pungent.

5. In the bowl of a food processor, combine the tea leaves, garlic, ginger, dried chiles, and fish sauce and blitz until the leaves are finely chopped. Keep the food processor going and drizzle in the lime juice and vegetable oil until a paste forms. Taste and adjust the seasonings if desired.

6. Pour the dressing back into the small container (from step 4) and store in the refrigerator for at least 3 more days for the flavors to meld.

7. To serve, toss the tea leaf salad dressing with the cabbage, tomatoes, cilantro, peanuts, sunflower seeds, and sesame seeds. Add more fish sauce or salt to taste and drizzle with the sesame oil. Serve with a wedge of lime or lemon.

   INGREDIENT TIP: Laphet (also spelled *lephet* or *lahpet*) are the fermented leaves of the tea plant (*Camellia sinensis*). Fresh tea leaves are steamed, then hand-mashed on bamboo mats. The mashed tea leaves are packed into a vessel, then weighted and fermented for several months to 1 year.

SOY-PICKLED BITTER MELON

JAPAN

Makes: 1 quart | **Prep time:** 10 minutes | **Pickling time:** 1 hour

1 pound Chinese bitter melons
(2 long melons)

¼ cup soy sauce

3 tablespoons rice vinegar

1 teaspoon sugar

1 (2-inch) square piece of
kombu (dried kelp, optional)

1 small dried red chile pepper,
like chile de arbol

Bitter melon, or bitter gourd, may just be the most bitter among all fruits and vegetables. It is a tropical vine in the gourd family and related to zucchini, squash, cucumber, and pumpkin. Despite its bitterness, bitter melon is popular in Asian cooking and has long been used to treat diabetes-related conditions. There are two types: the long, pale green Chinese variety that has smooth bumps and the narrower Indian one that has spiky skin and pointed ends. This recipe uses the former.

1. Halve the bitter melons lengthwise and scoop out the seeds. Cut crosswise into ½-inch slices.

2. In a zip-top bag, combine the soy sauce, vinegar, and sugar. Seal and shake to mix. Add the bitter melon, kombu (if using), and chile and gently massage. Expel as much air as possible from the bag, seal, and refrigerate for at least 1 hour. The bitter melon will keep for 1 week in the refrigerator.

CITRUS CHILE PASTE | YUZU KOSHO

JAPAN
Makes: 1 cup | **Prep time:** 20 minutes | **Curing time:** 2 to 3 days

6 Meyer lemons,
   preferably organic

2 large limes,
   preferably organic

3 jalapeño peppers, minced
   with seeds

1 teaspoon coarse sea salt or
   kosher salt

As its name implies, yuzu kosho is a condiment made with a Japanese citrus called yuzu and peppers (kosho). Yuzu is believed to be a hybrid of mandarin orange and ichang papeda (a group of citrus plants native to tropical Asia). It looks like a small grapefruit with a rough peel and is yellow when ripe. While yuzu is rarely eaten as a fruit, its tart and aromatic juice and zest are used in the same way lemons are used in other cuisines. The juice tastes like grapefruit with mandarin overtones. Yuzu is the main ingredient in Japanese ponzu sauce, and it is also made into yuzu vinegar.

Yuzu fruit is almost impossible to find fresh in the United States, although bottled juice is available. Meyer lemons, with their sweet-tart flavor and fragrance, make an excellent substitute, but if you can't find them, look for thin-skinned lemons and instead of 6 tablespoons lemon juice, use 4 tablespoons lemon juice and 2 tablespoons orange juice in this recipe.

1. Zest the lemons and limes with a Microplane grater until you get about ½ cup of zest. Juice the lemons to get 6 tablespoons of juice. (Save the remaining lemons and limes to use another time.)

2. In the bowl of a food processor, combine the zest, juice, jalapeños, and salt, and blitz until you have a coarse, yellowish-green paste. Or use a mortar and pestle. Transfer to a jar and cap tightly. Keep at room temperature and away from direct sunlight for 2 to 3 days to allow the flavors to develop. Store the yuzu kosho in the refrigerator, and it will keep for 1 to 2 months.

TRY IT WITH: Use yuzu kosho in a marinade (honey, ginger, and olive oil sound good), rub it on grilled meats or seafood like fish or scallops, or stir it into ramen or miso soup. When mixed into mayo, it becomes a zingy dip for French fries.

CHILI OIL

CHINA

Makes: ½ cup | **Prep and Cook time:** 10 minutes | **Infusing time:** 1 day

1 star anise pod

1 (1-inch) cinnamon stick

1 teaspoon sesame seeds

½ teaspoon Sichuan
peppercorns

2 tablespoons Asian red
pepper flakes, like Sichuan
chili flakes or Korean red
pepper flakes (gochujaru)

½ cup vegetable oil,
like peanut, sunflower,
grapeseed, or avocado

½ teaspoon coarse sea salt or
kosher salt

¼ teaspoon sugar

Sure, you can buy chili oil—or you can make your own, and adjust the heat level and balance of spices to your liking. This is a crucial ingredient for the Bamboo Shoots with Chili Oil (page 135), or you can drizzle it over noodles and rice for an instant pick-me-up.

1. In a small skillet (I use a cast-iron pan) over medium heat, dry roast the star anise, cinnamon stick, sesame seeds, and Sichuan peppercorns until fragrant and brown, 2 to 3 minutes. Stir often and watch carefully that the spices don't burn. Transfer the star anise and cinnamon stick to a medium heatproof bowl and add the red pepper flakes. Grind the Sichuan peppercorns and sesame seeds with a mortar and pestle or a spice grinder and add to the bowl.

2. In a small saucepan over medium-high heat, warm the oil until it starts to shimmer and bubble gently. Remove from the heat and carefully pour into the bowl with the spices. The spices will crackle and pop. Stir in the salt and sugar. Set aside to cool and let the spices infuse the oil for at least 1 day. Fish out the star anise and cinnamon before serving.

3. Use 3 tablespoons in Spicy Bamboo Shoots with Chili Oil (page 135) and save the remainder for another use. The chili oil will keep at room temperature for 2 weeks or in the refrigerator for 6 months.

SPICY BAMBOO SHOOTS IN CHILI OIL

CHINA

Makes: 1 cup | **Prep time:** 30 minutes | **Curing time:** 1 hour

1 cup shredded bamboo shoots
3 tablespoons homemade Chili Oil (page 134)
¼ teaspoon sesame oil
Pinch salt
Dash white pepper

Bamboo shoots are the tender shoots of the bamboo plant, harvested before they reach 1 foot tall. They are available fresh (and raw), canned, or vacuum-packed. Raw bamboo shoots contain toxins (cyanogenic glycosides), but these toxins can be easily destroyed by boiling the shoots in salted water for 15 to 20 minutes. I usually buy canned, because they're available everywhere, I can get them cut in just the size and shape I need (whether shredded or sliced), and they're ready-to-eat.

1. Rinse the bamboo shoots under cold running water. Drain in a colander and pat dry with a kitchen towel.

2. Transfer the bamboo shoots to a bowl and add the chili oil, using as much or as little of the chili flakes as you like. Add the sesame oil, salt, and pepper. Stir to combine. Taste and adjust the seasonings as desired.

3. Set aside for 1 hour for the flavors to meld before serving. To store, pack the bamboo shoots into an airtight container and store in the refrigerator for up to 1 week.

TRY IT WITH: Spicy bamboo shoots are delicious as a condiment served with fried rice or congee or eaten as a snack straight up. You can also add them to a stir-fry dish.

SALT-CURED EGGS

CHINA
Makes: 6 eggs | Prep and Cook time: 20 minutes | Curing time: 4 to 6 weeks

6 duck eggs or extra-large
  chicken eggs
2 cups water
½ cup coarse sea salt or
  kosher salt
2 teaspoons Chinese rice
  cooking wine
2 teaspoons sugar

In Chinese cuisine, cured egg yolks (curing uses 15 to 20 percent concentrated salt brine) are traditionally used in fillings for mooncakes, steamed buns, and egg custards. Duck eggs are favored for their fattier flavor, but you can use chicken eggs, too. Use a ratio of 1 cup of salt to 4 cups of water to adjust the formula for the number of eggs you'd like to cure. Additionally, feel free to add herbs and spices such as star anise, ginger, or cardamom for extra flavor and aroma. Cooking wine and sugar help the yolks obtain a bright orange color.

1. Wash all your equipment with hot, soapy water. Wash the eggs under cold running water and set aside to dry.

2. In a large saucepan over medium-high heat, combine the water and salt and bring to a boil. Stir until the salt dissolves completely. Adjust the heat and simmer for 3 to 5 minutes. Remove from the heat and stir in the wine and sugar until the sugar dissolves completely.

3. Place the eggs in a quart-size jar and pour in the brine. Place a weight (see page 14 for options) on top of the eggs to keep them submerged under the brine. Cap the jar tightly and cure at room temperature away from direct sunlight for 4 to 6 weeks.

4. After about 4 weeks, take an egg out to test for saltiness. Bring a small saucepan of water to a boil. Lower the egg gently into the water (their shells are thinner and more fragile than chicken eggs) and cook for 9 minutes. Prepare a bowl with ice water and place the egg into the bowl to chill after cooking. Leave to cool before peeling. This prevents a gray tinge from forming on the yolk's edge. A good-quality salted egg

should have a firm, bright-orange yolk, and the egg white should be pure white, not cloudy or yellow, and should have no off smell.

5. If the egg isn't salty enough, leave the rest in the brine for another week or two. Once the eggs are salty enough to your liking, drain them and store them in the refrigerator until you are ready to cook them. Salt-cured eggs will keep in the refrigerator for 3 to 4 weeks.

TRY IT WITH: Salt-cured eggs can be served smothered in sambal as a side dish with rice or noodles or eaten with congee. The yolks can be mashed and turned into a carbonara-like sauce for pasta. They can also be used as a filling for Chinese mooncakes and cookies.

PICKLED SUNCHOKES

FUSION

Makes: 1 quart | Prep time: 15 minutes, plus 3 to 8 hours brining time | Cook time: 30 minutes |
Pickling time: 1 to 3 days

FOR THE VEGETABLES

1 pound sunchokes (preferably small ones)

Juice of 1 lemon mixed with 3 cups water

FOR THE SALT BRINE

4 cups water

¼ cup coarse sea salt or kosher salt

FOR THE PICKLING LIQUID

1 cup cider vinegar

½ cup water

⅔ cup sugar

1 small fresh turmeric root, cut into 4 slices, or 1 teaspoon ground turmeric

2 dried chiles de arbol

2 teaspoons coriander seed

Sunchokes, or Jerusalem artichokes, are edible tubers (like potatoes). They are the thickened underground part of a certain breed of sunflower. The knobby root vegetables have light-brown skin, which may be tinged with yellow, red, or purple, depending on the soil they were grown in. Sunchokes are available year-round, but their prime season is October to April. Every fall and winter, I get a boatload of sunchokes in my CSA box. Other than roasting them, I didn't really know what to do with them until I discovered that they can be eaten raw and decided to pickle them! Peeling them is close to impossible because of their bumpy surface, so I usually eat them skin-on, which is a plus because the skin contains most of the nutrients.

1. **PREP THE SUNCHOKES:** Scrub the sunchokes well with a vegetable brush to remove any dirt and stringy bits. Cut them crosswise into ¼-inch slices and dunk them into the bowl of lemon water to prevent them from browning.

2. **MAKE THE SALT BRINE:** In a medium saucepan over medium-high heat, bring the water and salt to a boil. Stir until the salt dissolves completely. Set aside to cool. When the brine is cooled to room temperature, drain the sunchokes, and combine them with the brine in a large bowl. Cover and set aside for at least 3 hours, preferably 8 hours.

3. **MAKE THE PICKLING LIQUID:** In a medium saucepan over medium-high heat, combine the vinegar, water, sugar, turmeric, and dried chiles and bring to a boil. Stir until the sugar dissolves completely. Taste and adjust the seasonings if desired. Set aside to cool to room temperature.

4. Drain the sunchokes and rinse under cold running water. Drain in a colander. Pack the sunchokes into 2 pint-size jars. Fish out the turmeric slices and dried chiles from the pickling liquid. Slip 2 turmeric slices, 1 dried chile, and 1 teaspoon coriander seed into each jar. Pour the cooled pickling liquid over the sunchokes, leaving ½ inch of headspace. Cap the jars and store in the refrigerator for 1 to 3 days before eating. The sunchokes will keep in the refrigerator for 2 weeks.

YES YOU CAN! Pickled sunchokes can be canned so they keep for up to 1 year on the shelf. Feel free to double or triple the recipe. Following the canning instructions on page 15, place the sunchokes in 2 hot, pint-size jars that have been washed in hot, soapy water. Fill the jars with hot pickling liquid, leaving a ¼-inch headspace. Remove any air bubbles, wipe the rims, and seal the jars. Process in a water-bath canner for 15 minutes. Wait 5 minutes before removing the jars, and check the seals after 12 to 24 hours.

INGREDIENT TIP: Fresh turmeric is available at Asian and Indian markets, as well as at specialty grocery stores like Whole Foods. Use extra turmeric to make golden milk by steeping slices in your choice of hot milk (coconut is wonderful) with black pepper for a comforting, healing beverage.

PICKLED CHAYOTE

SOUTHEAST ASIAN-INSPIRED
Makes: 1 quart | Prep and Cook time: 10 minutes | Pickling time: 2 to 3 days

FOR THE VEGETABLES
13 ounces to 1 pound chayote
  (1 medium chayote)
1 jalapeño, chopped (optional)

FOR THE BRINE
½ cup vinegar
½ cup soy sauce
½ cup water
½ cup sugar

Chayote squash, also called mirliton or vegetable pear, is a summer squash that originates in Mexico. Chayote looks like a large pear and has the crunchy texture of unripe pear with a mild, almost cucumber-like flavor. Today, it grows in many warm climates all over the world, including Southeast Asia. My mom used to cut chayote into matchsticks and stir-fry it with baby shrimp. Imagine my surprise when I discovered that chayote could be pickled and even eaten raw. Chayote is a very nutritious fruit-vegetable, but most of the nutrients are in the peel, so try to cook and eat it peel-on!

1. **PREP THE VEGETABLES:** If you decide to peel the chayote, wear food-safe gloves. Chayote releases a slimy sap when peeled that can irritate your skin. Rinse the peeled chayote under cold running water and pat dry.

2. Halve the chayote lengthwise and cut crosswise into ¼-inch-thick slices. Pack into a quart-size jar with the chopped jalapeño, if using.

3. **MAKE THE BRINE:** In a small saucepan over medium heat, combine the vinegar, soy sauce, water, and sugar, and bring to a boil. Remove from the heat and set aside to cool for a few minutes. Pour the brine over the chayote in the jar.

4. Cool at room temperature and store in the refrigerator for 2 to 3 days before serving. The pickled chayote will keep for 2 weeks in the refrigerator.

INGREDIENT TIP: Chayote is available at Asian and Latino markets. Look for a fruit that's firm to the touch, between light and dark green in color, and without any blemishes or off-color soft spots.

PICKLED PEANUTS | LAO CU HUASHENG

CHINA
Makes: 1½ cups | Prep time: 10 minutes

3 tablespoons balsamic
  vinegar, preferably
  nicely aged
3 tablespoons soy sauce
1 tablespoon honey
2 teaspoons sesame oil
Pinch salt
1 cup unsalted
  roasted peanuts
½ cup finely chopped red
  onion (½ medium onion)

Pickled peanuts? Yes! It's a popular snack and appetizer in China and is a very simple dish. The Chinese name "lao cu huasheng" means old vinegar peanuts. I believe that the vinegar used is traditionally an aged black vinegar like Chinkiang black vinegar. I've adapted the recipe here to use balsamic vinegar, which you are more likely to have in your pantry. You can also add cilantro, celery, or chiles to the mix. Refreshing and crunchy, pickled peanuts are a snack you'll be popping all day long.

In a medium bowl, stir together the vinegar, soy sauce, honey, sesame oil, and salt. Add the peanuts and onion and toss to coat evenly. Taste and adjust the seasonings if desired. The peanuts are ready to eat immediately, but if you set them aside for a few hours to allow the flavors to meld together, they will taste much better.

INGREDIENT TIP: If you can find them, buy peanuts with their red skins still on (like Spanish peanuts), because they will make this dish more authentic. These nuts are usually sold raw. To roast them, preheat the oven to 350°F and spread the peanuts on a large baking sheet. Bake for 8 minutes, then turn off the heat and leave the peanuts in the oven until they cool down.

SALTY LIMEADE | CHANH MUỐI

VIETNAM
Makes: 12 limes | Prep and Cook time: 10 minutes | Fermenting time: 3 weeks

2 cups water

¼ cup coarse sea salt or kosher salt, plus more to sprinkle

10 to 12 Key limes (or as many as can fit into a quart-size jar), preferably organic

Superfine sugar, for serving

Still water, sparkling water, or lemon-lime soda like 7-Up, for serving

Salty lemonade or limeade is a popular "soda" in Vietnam. To make it, the citrus fruit is first preserved in brine. The preserved fruit and the drink go by the same name, "chanh muối." The fruit is also used as a home remedy for colds: Simply steep a wedge in a cup of hot water and stir in some honey.

1. Wash all your equipment with hot, soapy water.

2. In a small saucepan over medium-high heat, bring the water to a boil. Stir in the salt until it dissolves completely. Remove from the heat and set aside to cool.

3. Scrub the limes to remove any wax or dirt. Cut off the top and bottom ends of the limes to reveal some flesh. Halve them partway, not all the way through. You want them to stay attached at one end.

4. Sprinkle salt inside each lime and pack into a quart-size jar. Pour in the brine, leaving a headspace of 1 inch. Place a weight (see page 14 for options) on top of the limes to keep them submerged under the brine. Cap loosely and ferment at room temperature in a sunny spot for at least 3 weeks. The limes may brown and the brine may turn cloudy, and that's okay. The limes will keep at room temperature indefinitely. Always use a clean utensil to scoop out the limes.

5. To make the limeade, place a salted lime in a tall glass. Muddle with a spoon. Add the sugar to taste and pour in the water or soda. Stir until the sugar dissolves. The limeade should have a subtle salty-sweet flavor.

SWITCH THINGS UP: Try curing Meyer lemons and kumquats, too. Or muddle the lime with mint.

PICKLED SWEET POTATOES

FUSION

Makes: 1 quart | Prep and Cook time: 20 minutes, plus 1 hour sitting time | Pickling time: 1 hour

1 pound sweet potatoes (2 to 3 medium potatoes)

½ jalapeño, seeded and chopped

1 cup distilled white vinegar

1 cup water

¼ cup sugar

1 teaspoon coarse sea salt or kosher salt

½ teaspoon freshly ground black pepper

1 (2-inch) piece fresh ginger, peeled and cut into thin slices

½ cup green onions, finely chopped (2 stalks)

My mom pickles just about everything. I remember biting into a hard orange chunk once thinking it was carrot. It wasn't. I don't recommend pickling chunks of sweet potato, but when they are sliced very thin, sweet potatoes make tasty, crunchy, and surprisingly good pickles. Use a mandoline if you have one. If not, a very sharp paring knife will do the job.

1. Peel the sweet potatoes and cut crosswise into very thin, round slices, about ¹⁄₁₆-inch thick. Use a mandoline if you have one. Soak the slices in a large bowl of cold water for at least 1 hour to remove excess starch. Rinse with cold running water and drain in a colander. Pat dry with kitchen towels.

2. In a medium nonreactive bowl, combine the sweet potatoes and jalapeño.

3. In a nonreactive saucepan over medium heat, combine the vinegar, water, sugar, salt, pepper, and ginger and bring to a boil. Adjust the heat and simmer for 2 minutes, stirring until the sugar dissolves completely. Remove from the heat and pour over the sweet potatoes.

4. Cover and set aside for 1 hour at room temperature to allow the flavors to meld. Just before serving, stir in the green onions. Keep leftovers in the refrigerator for up to 1 week.

DON'T FORGET: While sweet potatoes are edible raw, other potatoes are not. So don't try to substitute other potatoes in this recipe.

CHINESE FIVE-SPICE PICKLED GRAPES

ASIAN FUSION

Makes: 1 quart | Prep and Cook time: 15 minutes | Pickling time: 8 to 24 hours

1 pound seedless red or
  black grapes
1 cup apple cider vinegar
¼ cup water
¾ cup sugar
Pinch salt
1 (2-inch) cinnamon stick
1 star anise pod
½ teaspoon fennel seeds
⅛ teaspoon Sichuan
  peppercorns
5 whole cloves

Chinese five-spice is very much like French herbes de Provence, a blend of herbs and spices that is strongly associated with the region's cuisine. The spices and amounts in the five-spice blend vary from region to region and even from household to household. It all depends on personal tastes and preferences. However, the most common ingredients are cinnamon, star anise, fennel seeds, Sichuan peppercorns, and cloves. If you already have ground Chinese five-spice powder in your pantry, use 2 teaspoons for your pickling brine.

1. Remove the grapes from the stem and halve them.

2. In a medium saucepan over medium-high heat, combine the vinegar, water, sugar, and salt, and bring to a boil. Remove from the heat and set aside to cool.

3. In a quart-size jar, place the cinnamon, star anise, fennel seeds, peppercorns, and cloves. Add the grapes. Pour the cooled brine over the grapes. I like to cool the brine before pouring it over the grapes so they stay firm. You can pour hot brine over the grapes to yield a more tender pickle, and the grapes will absorb the flavors faster. The choice is yours.

4. Cap the jar and store the pickled grapes in the refrigerator for at least 8 to 24 hours before serving cold. The grapes will keep in the refrigerator for 1 month.

YES YOU CAN! The pickled grapes can be canned so they keep for up to 1 year on the shelf. Feel free to double or triple the recipe. Following the canning instructions on page 15, place the grapes in hot jars that have been washed with hot, soapy water, leaving a 1-inch headspace. Fill the jars with hot brine, leaving a ½-inch headspace. Remove any air bubbles, wipe the rims, and seal the jars. Process in a water-bath canner for 15 minutes (pints) or 20 minutes (quarts). Wait 5 minutes before removing the jars, and check the seals after 12 to 24 hours.

SEVEN GODS CURRY PICKLE | FUKUJINZUKE

JAPAN

Makes: 1 quart | **Prep time:** 15 minutes, plus 30 minutes sitting time | **Cook time:** 10 minutes | **Pickling time:** 4 days to 1 week

FOR THE VEGETABLES

¾ cup diced cucumber
  (4 ounces)
¾ cup peeled and diced
  daikon radish (3 ounces)
½ cup peeled and diced carrot
  (2 ounces)
½ cup diced Japanese
  eggplant (3 ounces)
1 tablespoon coarse sea salt or
  kosher salt
½ cup peeled and chopped
  lotus root (2 ounces)

FOR THE MARINADE

6 tablespoons soy sauce
¾ cup rice vinegar
¼ cup mirin
¼ cup sake or Chinese
  rice wine
3 tablespoons sugar
1 (3-inch) square piece kombu
  (dried kelp), soaked in water
  until soft and sliced into
  thin strips
1 teaspoon dried chili flakes,
  like togarashi

Fukujinzuke is a Japanese pickle made with soy sauce and vinegar that is often served with curry. With its acidic qualities and crunchy texture, it's a delightful contrast to soft, spicy curry. The name *fukujinzuke* pays homage to iconic figures from Japanese popular mythology: the Seven Gods of Good Fortune, or Shichi Fukujin. The pickle was traditionally made with seven vegetables, among them daikon radish, eggplant, lotus root, and cucumber. Other common ingredients include carrots, shiso, kombu, ginger, and sometimes beets for color.

1. PREP THE VEGETABLES: In a large bowl, toss the cucumber, daikon, carrot, and eggplant with the salt. Place a heavy plate on top of the vegetables to weigh them down, and set aside for at least 30 minutes.

2. Bring a small saucepan of water to a boil over medium-high heat. Rinse the lotus root in cold water. Add the lotus root to the boiling water. When the water returns to a boil, simmer for 1 minute. Drain the lotus root and set aside.

3. After 30 minutes, remove the weight from the vegetables. Rinse with cold running water and drain in a colander. With clean hands, take a handful at a time and squeeze as much water as you can from the vegetables. Transfer them to another bowl. Discard all the liquid.

4. **MAKE THE MARINADE:** In a medium saucepan over medium-high heat, bring the soy sauce, vinegar, mirin, sake, and sugar to a boil. Adjust the heat to a simmer and add the vegetables and lotus root. Once the liquid starts to simmer again, remove from the heat and set aside to cool.

5. Scoop out the vegetables with a slotted spoon or spider and pack into a quart-size jar.

6. Return the marinade to the stove and bring back to a boil. Remove from the heat and add the kombu and chili flakes. Set aside to cool to room temperature, then pour over the vegetables. Cap the jar and store in the refrigerator for 4 to 5 days. Taste and see whether it is pickled to your liking. The pickle will taste best after at least 1 week. It will keep in the refrigerator for 4 to 5 weeks.

SWITCH IT UP: The only rule you need to follow for this recipe is that you need 1 pound of vegetables, about 3 cups chopped. The list of vegetables in the recipe is just a guideline. You can use whatever vegetables are in season or in your kitchen!

ALL ABOUT ALTITUDE

It takes longer for water to boil at higher altitudes, because the air pressure is lower. Water evaporates faster, and gases expand more at higher altitudes as well. For those of you living at higher altitudes, chances are you have already learned to adjust your cooking and baking recipes. With water-bath canning, you simply have to extend the processing time slightly at higher elevations. Use this chart to make the necessary adjustments. If you don't know your altitude, check out the chart on the following pages.

WATER-BATH CANNING ADJUSTMENTS

ALTITUDE IN FEET	INCREASE PROCESSING TIME
0–1,000	No adjustment needed
1,001–3,000	5 minutes
3,001–6,000	10 minutes
6,001–8,000	15 minutes
8,001–10,000	20 minutes

ALTITUDES OF CITIES IN THE UNITED STATES AND CANADA

United States

STATE	CITY	FEET	METERS
Arizona	Mesa	1,243	379
	Phoenix	1,150	351
	Scottsdale	1,257	383
	Tucson	2,389	728
California	Fontana	1,237	377
	Moreno Valley	1,631	497
Colorado	Aurora	5,471	1,668
	Colorado Springs	6,010	1,832
	Denver	5,183	1,580
Georgia	Atlanta	1,026	313
Idaho	Boise	2,730	832
	Idaho Falls	4,705	1,434
Iowa	Sioux City	1,201	366
Kansas	Wichita	1,299	396
Montana	Billings	3,123	952
	Missoula	3,209	978
Nebraska	Henderson	1,867	569
	Lincoln	1,176	358
	Omaha	1,090	332
Nevada	Las Vegas	2,001	610
	Reno	4,505	1,373
New Mexico	Albuquerque	5,312	1,619
	Santa Fe	7,260	2,213
North Carolina	Asheville	2,134	650
North Dakota	Bismarck	1,686	514
Ohio	Akron	1,004	306

STATE	CITY	FEET	METERS
Oklahoma	Oklahoma City	1,201	366
Pennsylvania	Pittsburgh	1,370	418
South Dakota	Rapid City	3,202	976
Texas	Amarillo	3,605	1,099
	El Paso	3,740	1,140
	Lubbock	3,256	992
Utah	Provo	4,551	1,387
	Salt Lake City	4,226	1,288
Washington	Spokane	1,843	562
Wyoming	Casper	5,150	1,570

Canada

PROVINCE	CITY	FEET	METERS
Alberta	Calgary	3,600	1,100
	Edmonton	2,201	671
Ontario	Hamilton	1,063	324
Manitoba	Brandon	1,313	409
Saskatchewan	Regina	1,893	577
	Saskatoon	1,580	482

MEASUREMENT CONVERSIONS

VOLUME EQUIVALENTS (LIQUID)

US STANDARD	US STANDARD (OUNCES)	METRIC (APPROXIMATE)
2 tablespoons	1 fl. oz.	30 mL
¼ cup	2 fl. oz.	60 mL
½ cup	4 fl. oz.	120 mL
1 cup	8 fl. oz.	240 mL
1½ cups	12 fl. oz.	355 mL
2 cups or 1 pint	16 fl. oz.	475 mL
4 cups or 1 quart	32 fl. oz.	1 L
1 gallon or 4 quarts	128 fl. oz.	4 L

VOLUME EQUIVALENTS (DRY)

US STANDARD	METRIC (APPROXIMATE)
⅛ teaspoon	0.5 mL
¼ teaspoon	1 mL
½ teaspoon	2 mL
¾ teaspoon	4 mL
1 teaspoon	5 mL
1 tablespoon	15 mL
¼ cup	59 mL
⅓ cup	79 mL
½ cup	118 mL
⅔ cup	156 mL
¾ cup	177 mL
1 cup	235 mL
2 cups or 1 pint	475 mL
3 cups	700 mL
4 cups or 1 quart	1 L

OVEN TEMPERATURES

FAHRENHEIT	CELSIUS (APPROXIMATE)
250°F	120°C
300°F	150°C
325°F	165°C
350°F	180°C
375°F	190°C
400°F	200°C
425°F	220°C
450°F	230°C

WEIGHT EQUIVALENTS

US STANDARD	METRIC (APPROXIMATE)
½ ounce	15 g
1 ounce	30 g
2 ounces	60 g
4 ounces	115 g
8 ounces	225 g
12 ounces	340 g
16 ounces or 1 pound	455 g

RESOURCES

AMAZON.COM

A wide variety of nonperishable Asian ingredients and cookware are available on Amazon.

IMPORTFOOD.COM

A great resource for Southeast Asian ingredients, both fresh and packaged.

MELISSAS.COM

Melissa's Produce imports and distributes exotic fresh fruits and vegetables from around the globe.

TOKYOCENTRAL.COM

A hub for Japanese groceries and goods.

REFERENCES

BOOKS

The All New Ball Book of Canning and Preserving (Oxmoor House, 2016)

The Art of Fermentation: An In-Depth Exploration of Essential Concepts and Processes from Around the World by Sandor Ellix Katz (Chelsea Green Publishing, 2012)

Asian Pickles: Sweet, Sour, Salty, Cured, and Fermented Preserves by Karen Solomon (Ten Speed Press, 2014)

Japanese Pickled Vegetables: 129 Homestyle Recipes for Traditional Brined, Vinegared and Fermented Pickles by Machiko Tateno (Tuttle Publishing, 2019)

The Korean Kimchi Cookbook: 78 Fiery Recipes for Korea's Legendary Pickled and Fermented Vegetables by Kim Man-Jo, Lee O-Young, and Lee Kyou-Tae (Tuttle Publishing, 2018)

WEBSITES

Colorado State University Extension: farmtotable.colostate.edu

Diane M. Barrett, "Maximizing the Nutritional Value of Fruits and Vegetables": fruitandvegetable.ucdavis.edu/files/197179.pdf

National Center for Home Food Preservation: nchfp.uga.edu/publications /publications_usda.html

RECIPES BY COUNTRY

C

China

Chili Oil, 134

Fermented White Tofu (Bai Fu Ru), 76–77

Pickled Peanuts (Lao Cu Huasheng), 141

Plum Sauce (or Duck Sauce), 73

Quick Cucumber and Carrot Pickles, 27

Salt-Cured Eggs, 136–137

Salt-Pickled Mustard Cabbage
(Suan Cai), 108–109

Sichuan Pickles (Pao Cai), 110

Spicy Bamboo Shoots in Chili Oil, 135

Spicy Smacked Cucumbers (Suan
La Pai Huang Gua), 38–39

Sweet-and-Sour Chinese Mustard
Cabbage Pickle, 30

I

India

Cilantro-Mint Chutney, 65

Fiery Lime Pickle (Nimbu Ka Achaar),
70–71

Green Mango Pickle, 66–67

Honey-Pickled Chickpeas, 126

Lime Juice Pickle, 60–61

Mango Chutney, 63

Spiced Chickpea Pickle, 127

Sweet, Sour, and Spicy Mango
Sauce (Amba), 68–69

Tomato-Date Chutney, 64

Indonesia

Indonesian Chile Paste (Sambal Oelek), 57

Indonesian Fruit Salad (Asinan Buah), 32

Mum's Mixed Pickle (Acar Campur), 37

Shrimp Paste Sambal (Sambal Terasi),
58–59

Turmeric-Spiced Pickles (Acar Kuning),
34–35

Israel

Sweet, Sour, and Spicy Mango
Sauce (Amba), 68–69

J

Japan

Citrus Chile Paste (Yuzu Kosho), 133

Fermented Yellow Radish (Takuan), 102–103

Miso-Cured Daikon (Misozuke), 29

Miso-Ginger Sauerkraut, 114–115

Pickled Ginger (Gari), 42–43

Rice Bran Pickles (Nukazuke), 96–98

Salted Rice Koji Pickles (Shio Koji
Asazuke), 104–105

Salt-Pickled Vegetables (Shiozuke), 48–49

Sesame Pickled Cabbage, 45

Seven Gods Curry Pickle
(Fukujinzuke), 146–147

Soy-Pickled Bitter Melon, 132

Soy-Pickled Mushrooms, 33

Soy Sauce-Pickled Eggs (Shoyu Tamago), 128

Spicy Pickled Lotus Root, 47

K

Korea

Apple and Celery Kimchi, 122–123

Bitter Greens Kimchi, 100

Broccoli Rabe Kimchi, 94–95

Classic Cabbage Kimchi (Baechu
Kimchi), 86–88

Daikon and Jicama Water Kimchi
(Dongchimi), 111

Easy Kimchi (Mak Kimchi), 90–91

Green Mango Pickle (Pa Kimchi), 89

Korean Red Pepper Paste (Gochujang), 80–81

Quick Cucumber Kimchi, 99

Red Vegetable Kimchi, 112–113

Sesame Zucchini Threads (Hobak Namul), 41

White Kimchi (Baek Kimchi), 92–93

M

Malaysia

Pineapple and Cucumber Relish
(Acar Nenas Dan Timun), 31

Myanmar
    Pickled Tea Leaf Dressing (Laphet
        Thoke), 130–131
    Shan Pickles (Mon-Nyin Chin), 106–107

N

Nepal
    Momo Sauce, 79

P

Philippines
    Banana Ketchup, 74–75
    Shredded Vegetable Pickles (Achara), 50–51

S

Singapore
    Lemongrass Chile Sauce, 78
    Pickled Green Chiles, 46
Sri Lanka
    Sri Lankan Chile Paste (Katta Sambol), 72

T

Taiwan
    Salt-Pickled Mustard Cabbage
        (Suan Cai), 108–109
    Sweet Cucumber Pickles (Hua Gua), 28
Thailand
    Pickled Shallots, 129
    Roasted Chile Jam (Nam Prik Pao), 56
    Thai Sweet Chile Sauce, 62

V

Vietnam
    Fermented Eggplant (Ca Phao Muoi),
        116–117
    Pickled Bean Sprouts (Du'a Gia), 44
    Pickled Daikon and Carrots (Do Chua), 26
    Salty Limeade (Chanh Muối), 142
    Sliced Papaya Pickles, 40
    Sweet and Spicy Pickled Baby Eggplant, 36

INDEX

A

Acar Campur, 37
Acar Kuning, 34–35
Acar Nenas Dan Timun, 31
Achara, 50–51
Altitude, 149–151
Amba, 68–69
Apple cider vinegar, 11
Apples
  Apple and Celery Kimchi,
    122–123
  White Kimchi, 92–93
Apricots
  Plum Sauce (or Duck Sauce), 73
Asafoetida, 12
Asian Pear and Fennel Pickles,
  124–125
Asinan Buah, 32

B

Bacteria, 3, 8
Baechu Kimchi, 86–88
Baek Kimchi, 92–93
Bai Fu Ru, 76–77
Bamboo Shoots in Chili Oil, Spicy, 135
Banana Ketchup, 74–75
Bean Sprouts, Pickled, 44
Beets
  Red Vegetable Kimchi, 112–113
Bitter Greens Kimchi, 100
Bitter Melon, Soy-Pickled, 132
Brining, 2–3
Broccoli
  Salted Rice Koji Pickles, 104–105
Broccoli Rabe Kimchi, 94–95

C

Cabbage. See also Mustard cabbage
  Classic Cabbage Kimchi, 86–88
  Easy Kimchi, 90–91
  Miso-Ginger Sauerkraut, 114–115
  Mum's Mixed Pickle, 37
  Pickled Tea Leaf Dressing, 130–131
  Red Vegetable Kimchi, 112–113
  Sesame Pickled Cabbage, 45
  Sichuan Pickles, 110
  White Kimchi, 92–93
Canning, 15–17, 149–151
Canning salt, 10
Ca Phao Muoi, 116–117
Carrots
  Bitter Greens Kimchi, 100
  Classic Cabbage Kimchi, 86–88
  Miso-Ginger Sauerkraut, 114–115
  Mum's Mixed Pickle, 37
  Pickled Bean Sprouts, 44
  Pickled Daikon and Carrots, 26
  Quick Cucumber and Carrot Pickles, 27
  Rice Bran Pickles, 96–98
  Salted Rice Koji Pickles, 104–105
  Salt-Pickled Vegetables, 48–49
  Sesame Zucchini Threads, 41
  Seven Gods Curry Pickle, 146–147
  Shan Pickles, 106–107
  Shredded Vegetable Pickles, 50–51
  Sichuan Pickles, 110
  Turmeric-Spiced Pickles, 34–35
Cauliflower
  Mum's Mixed Pickle, 37
  Sichuan Pickles, 110
  Turmeric-Spiced Pickles, 34–35
Celery
  Apple and Celery Kimchi,
    122–123
  Sichuan Pickles, 110
Chanh Muối, 142
Chayote, Pickled, 140
Chickpeas
  Honey-Pickled Chickpeas, 126
  Spiced Chickpea Pickle, 127

Chiles, 11
    Banana Ketchup, 74–75
    Cilantro-Mint Chutney, 65
    Honey-Pickled Chickpeas, 126
    Indonesian Chile Paste, 57
    Lemongrass Chile Sauce, 78
    Mango Chutney, 63
    Momo Sauce, 79
    Pickled Bean Sprouts, 44
    Pickled Green Chiles, 46
    Pickled Shallots, 129
    Pickled Tea Leaf Dressing, 130–131
    Pineapple and Cucumber Relish, 31
    Plum Sauce (or Duck Sauce), 73
    Rice Bran Pickles, 96–98
    Roasted Chile Jam, 56
    Sesame Zucchini Threads, 41
    Shredded Vegetable Pickles, 50–51
    Shrimp Paste Sambal, 58–59
    Sichuan Pickles, 110
    Sliced Papaya Pickles, 40
    Sri Lankan Chile Paste, 72
    Sweet and Spicy Pickled Baby Eggplant, 36
    Sweet, Sour, and Spicy Mango Sauce,
        68–69
    Thai Sweet Chile Sauce, 62
    Tomato-Date Chutney, 64
    Turmeric-Spiced Pickles, 34–35
Chili Oil, 134
China, 120–121. See also Recipes
        by Country Index
Chinese Five-Spice Pickled Grapes, 144–145
Chutneys
    Mango Chutney, 63
    Tomato-Date Chutney, 64
Cilantro
    Cilantro-Mint Chutney, 65
    Momo Sauce, 79
    Pickled Tea Leaf Dressing, 130–131
Citrus, 11
Citrus Chile Paste, 133
Classic Cabbage Kimchi, 86–88
Cucumbers, 11
    Mum's Mixed Pickle, 37
    Pineapple and Cucumber Relish, 31

Quick Cucumber and Carrot Pickles, 27
Quick Cucumber Kimchi, 99
Rice Bran Pickles, 96–98
Salt-Pickled Vegetables, 48–49
Seven Gods Curry Pickle, 146–147
Spicy Smacked Cucumbers, 38–39
Sweet Cucumber Pickles, 28
Turmeric-Spiced Pickles, 34–35
Curing, 19
Curry leaves, 12

D

Daikon radishes
    Classic Cabbage Kimchi, 86–88
    Daikon and Jicama Water Kimchi, 111
    Fermented Yellow Radish, 102–103
    Miso-Cured Daikon, 29
    Pickled Daikon and Carrots, 26
    Salted Rice Koji Pickles, 104–105
    Salt-Pickled Vegetables, 48–49
    Seven Gods Curry Pickle, 146–147
    White Kimchi, 92–93
Dates
    Tomato-Date Chutney, 64
    White Kimchi, 92–93
Do Chua, 26
Dongchimi, 111
Du'a Gia, 44

E

Easy Kimchi, 90–91
Eggplants, 12
    Fermented Eggplant, 116–117
    Seven Gods Curry Pickle, 146–147
    Sweet and Spicy Pickled Baby Eggplant, 36
Eggs
    Salt-Cured Eggs, 136–137
    Soy Sauce-Pickled Eggs, 128
Equipment, 14–15

F

Fennel and Asian Pear Pickles, 124–125
Fenugreek, 12
Fermentation, 2–3, 17–19
Fermented Eggplant, 116–117

Fermented White Tofu, 76–77
Fermented Yellow Radish, 102–103
Fiery Lime Pickle, 70–71
Fish sauce, 13
Fukujinzuke, 146–147

G

Gari, 42–43
Ginger
 Miso-Ginger Sauerkraut, 114–115
 Pickled Ginger, 42–43
Gochujang, 80–81
Gochujaru, 12
Grapes, Chinese Five-Spice Pickled, 144–145
Green beans
 Salted Rice Koji Pickles, 104–105
Green Mango Pickle, 66–67
Green Onion Kimchi, 89
Greens
 Bitter Greens Kimchi, 100
 Shan Pickles, 106–107

H

Hobak Namul, 41
Honey-Pickled Chickpeas, 126
Hua Gua, 28

I

India, 54–55. *See also* Recipes by Country Index
Indonesian Chile Paste, 57
Indonesian Fruit Salad, 32

J

Japan, 6–7. *See also* Recipes by Country Index
Jicama
 Daikon and Jicama Water Kimchi, 111
 Indonesian Fruit Salad, 32
 Shredded Vegetable Pickles, 50–51

K

Kimchi
 Apple and Celery Kimchi, 122–123
 Bitter Greens Kimchi, 100
 Broccoli Rabe Kimchi, 94–95
 Classic Cabbage Kimchi, 86–88
 Daikon and Jicama Water Kimchi, 111
 Easy Kimchi, 90–91
 Green Onion Kimchi, 89
 Red Vegetable Kimchi, 112–113
 White Kimchi, 92–93
Kombu, 13
Korea, 84–85. *See also* Recipes by Country Index
Korean Red Pepper Paste, 80–81
Kosher salt, 10

L

Lactofermentation, 2–3, 17–19
Lao Cu Huasheng, 141
Laphet Thoke, 130–131
Lemongrass
 Lemongrass Chile Sauce, 78
 Pickled Shallots, 129
 Turmeric-Spiced Pickles, 34–35
Lemons
 Citrus Chile Paste, 133
Limes
 Citrus Chile Paste, 133
 Fiery Lime Pickle, 70–71
 Lime Juice Pickle, 60–61
 Salty Limeade, 142
Lotus root
 Seven Gods Curry Pickle, 146–147
 Spicy Pickled Lotus Root, 47

M

Mak Kimchi, 90–91
Mangos, 12
 Green Mango Pickle, 66–67
 Indonesian Fruit Salad, 32
 Mango Chutney, 63
 Sweet, Sour, and Spicy Mango Sauce,
  68–69
Mint-Cilantro Chutney, 65
Miso, 13
Miso-Cured Daikon, 29
Miso-Ginger Sauerkraut, 114–115
Misozuke, 29
Momo Sauce, 79
Mon-Nyin Chin, 106–107
Mum's Mixed Pickle, 37

Mushrooms
    Rice Bran Pickles, 96–98
    Soy-Pickled Mushrooms, 33
Mustard cabbage
    Salt-Pickled Mustard Cabbage, 108–109
    Sweet-and-Sour Chinese Mustard
        Cabbage Pickle, 30

N

Nam Prik Pao, 56
Nimbu Ka Achaar, 70–71
Nukazuke, 96–98
Nutrients, 8
Nuts
    Momo Sauce, 79
    Pickled Peanuts, 141
    Pickled Tea Leaf Dressing, 130–131
    Turmeric-Spiced Pickles, 34–35
    White Kimchi, 92–93

O

Oil, 3

P

Pa Kimchi, 89
Pao Cai, 110
Papayas, 12
    Shredded Vegetable Pickles, 50–51
    Sliced Papaya Pickles, 40
Pastes
    Citrus Chile Paste, 133
    Indonesian Chile Paste, 57
    Korean Red Pepper Paste, 80–81
    Roasted Chile Jam, 56
    Shrimp Paste Sambal, 58–59
Pears
    Asian Pear and Fennel Pickles,
        124–125
    White Kimchi, 92–93
Peppers
    Broccoli Rabe Kimchi, 94–95
    Citrus Chile Paste, 133
    Mum's Mixed Pickle, 37
    Pickled Sweet Potatoes, 143
    Salted Rice Koji Pickles, 104–105

Shredded Vegetable Pickles,
        50–51
    Turmeric-Spiced Pickles, 34–35
    White Kimchi, 92–93
Pickled Bean Sprouts, 44
Pickled Chayote, 140
Pickled Daikon and Carrots, 26
Pickled Ginger, 42–43
Pickled Green Chiles, 46
Pickled Peanuts, 141
Pickled Shallots, 129
Pickled Sunchokes, 138
Pickled Sweet Potatoes, 143
Pickled Tea Leaf Dressing, 130–131
Pickles and pickling
    defined, 2
    health benefits, 8–9
    history, 4
    steps, 1
    troubleshooting, 20
Pickling salt, 10
Pineapple
    Indonesian Fruit Salad, 32
    Pineapple and Cucumber Relish, 31
Plum Sauce (or Duck Sauce), 73
Probiotics, 8
Produce, 11–12

Q

Quick Cucumber and Carrot Pickles, 27
Quick Cucumber Kimchi, 99
Quick pickles, 2

R

Radishes. *See also* Daikon radishes
    Rice Bran Pickles, 96–98
    Sichuan Pickles, 110
Raisins
    Mango Chutney, 63
    Tomato-Date Chutney, 64
Red Vegetable Kimchi, 112–113
Rice Bran Pickles, 96–98
Rice flour, 13
Rice vinegar, 11
Roasted Chile Jam, 56

S

Salt, 2–3, 9, 10
Salt-Cured Eggs, 136–137
Salted Rice Koji Pickles, 104–105
Salt-Pickled Mustard Cabbage, 108–109
Salt-Pickled Vegetables, 48–49
Salty Limeade, 142
Sambal Oelek, 57
Sambal Terasi, 58–59
Sauces
  Banana Ketchup, 74–75
  Lemongrass Chile Sauce, 78
  Momo Sauce, 79
  Plum Sauce (or Duck Sauce), 73
  Sweet, Sour, and Spicy Mango Sauce,
    68–69
Sea salt, 10
Sesame Pickled Cabbage, 45
Sesame Zucchini Threads, 41
Seven Gods Curry Pickle, 146–147
Shallots, Pickled, 129
Shan Pickles, 106–107
Shio Koji Asazuke, 104–105
Shiozuke, 48–49
Shoyu Tamago, 128
Shredded Vegetable Pickles, 50–51
Shrimp Paste Sambal, 58–59
Sichuan Pickles, 110
Sliced Papaya Pickles, 40
Smells and odors, 19
Southeast Asia, 24–25. See also
    Recipes by Country Index
Soy-Pickled Bitter Melon, 132
Soy-Pickled Mushrooms, 33
Soy sauce, 13
Soy Sauce-Pickled Eggs, 128
Spiced Chickpea Pickle, 127
Spices, 3, 12
Spicy Bamboo Shoots in Chili Oil, 135
Spicy Pickled Lotus Root, 47

Spicy Smacked Cucumbers, 38–39
Sri Lankan Chile Paste, 72
Suan Cai, 108–109
Sugar, 3, 9
Sunchokes, Pickled, 138
Sweet-and-Sour Chinese Mustard
    Cabbage Pickle, 30
Sweet and Spicy Pickled Baby Eggplant, 36
Sweet Cucumber Pickles, 28
Sweet Potatoes, Pickled, 143
Sweet, Sour, and Spicy Mango Sauce, 68–69

T

Takuan, 102–103
Tea Leaf Dressing, Pickled, 130–131
Thai Sweet Chile Sauce, 62
Tofu, Fermented White, 76–77
Tomatoes
  Momo Sauce, 79
  Pickled Tea Leaf Dressing, 130–131
  Tomato-Date Chutney, 64
Tools, 14–15
Troubleshooting, 20
Turmeric-Spiced Pickles, 34–35
Turnips
  Rice Bran Pickles, 96–98

V

Vinegar, 2, 10–11

W

Water, 9
White Kimchi, 92–93
White vinegar, 11

Y

Yuzu Kosho, 133

Z

Zucchini Threads, Sesame, 41

ACKNOWLEDGMENTS

I'd like to express my gratitude to my editor Cecily McAndrews and developmental editor Caryn Abramowitz, for their keen eye for detail and unending patience on this project, as well as to the rest of the Callisto Media team for helping put together a beautiful book.

Endless thanks and infinite hugs and kisses go to my husband Omar and my son Isaac for their unending support and patience while I worked on this project, and especially for putting up with the various smells that emanated from the kitchen. I'm thrilled to have raised a pickle-loving son who is my partner in kimchi-eating crime!

ABOUT THE AUTHOR

Born in Indonesia and raised in Singapore, **PAT TANUMIHARDJA** has been a food and lifestyle writer for almost two decades. An expert on pan-Asian cuisine, Pat enjoys melding traditional Asian culinary styles with modern sensibilities. Her cookbooks include *Farm to Table Asian Secrets: Vegan and Vegetarian Full-Flavored Recipes for Every Season*, *The Asian Grandmothers Cookbook: Home Cooking from Asian American Kitchens*, and *Instant Pot Asian Pressure Cooker Meals: Fast, Fresh and Affordable*. Pat lives in Springfield, Virginia, with her husband and son. Find Pat on Twitter: @PicklesandTea, Instagram: @Pickles.and.Tea, and online: SmithsonianAPA.org/PicklesandTea.